FORWARD WITH COURAGE

FORWARD WITH COURAGE

Patsy Catherine Costanza

To order additional copies of this book, contact:
Xlibris Corporation
1-888-795-4274
www.Xlibris.com
Orders@Xlibris.com
42090

CONTENTS

Dedication

This book is dedicated to my husband and children, and my beloved Southern siblings: David, Azalea, Deloise, Labanda and Dovye.

Introduction to Author and Family

Patsy Catherine Thornton Costanza, daughter of Vertie Lee Thornton and Alvin Thornton, was born at home on the cold, frosty morning of November 10, 1937, delivered by a black mid-wife named Fanny Harris. We lived in the tiny village of Cross Roads in the little southern town of Athens, Louisiana, Claiborne Parish. Athens is located about 50 miles north of Shreveport.

Patsy married Roxie Denman Costanza, of Ambridge, Pennsylvania, on March 5, 1955 (a Yankee to all her southern relatives). The Civil War had ended long years before, but Southerners still weren't sure about those people up north.

In the rolling hills of Southwestern Pennsylvania, on a 40-acre farm in Beaver County, Pat and Rocky raised their family of four sons and one daughter. This Rebel Girl and Yankee Boy were married 47 years.

Douglas Stuart Harmon was my great-great-Grandfather on my mother's side of the family. His wife was Grace Cleora. Stuart died in the battle of Chickamauga (Civil War) on the state lines of Tennessee and Georgia.

Stuart's son, Matthew, married Susan Frances Cranford, born May 3, 1862 and died July 15, 1939.

Matthew and Susan's daughter, Grace, married William Harrison Lee (my grandparents). William was a descendant of the great Civil War General Robert E. Lee.

Vertie Mae Lee, daughter of Will and Grace, married Alvin C. Thornton (my parents).

Matthew and Susan Harmon, William and Grace Lee, and Vertie and Alvin Thornton are all buried in Tulip Cemetery, Claiborne Parrish, Athens, Louisiana. Needless to say, my roots are firmly planted in the red clay hills of Northern Louisiana.

My great-great-Grandfather and Grandmother, my Dad's Mother's Family: William "Billie" Wagner Woodall married Mamie Elizabeth Smith. They had five children:

1) Daniel Anderson Woodall
2) William Andrew J. Woodall
3) Rachel C.S.M.J. Woodall
4) James Henry Woodall
5) Charles Pinckney Woodall

My great-Grandfather, Daniel Anderson Woodall married Mary Catherine Phillips on March 23, 1860 by Rev. John Roper in Talbot County, Georgia, just before the Civil War.

I was named for this great-Grandmother. My middle name is Catherine.

Daniel and Catherine's ninth child was my Grandmother. Her complete name was Rachel Caroline Sarah (Sallie) Elizabeth Woodall. She married William "Will" Jackson Thornton on November 12, 1893 in Elmore County, Alabama. My Father, Alvin Coley Thornton, was their eighth child.

William Jackson Thornton's Father was Charles W. Thornton, born in 1826. He married Nancy Catherine Culpepper. Charles served in Company C 3125 Alabama Infantry during the Civil War. He was captured June 15, 1864 at Big Shanty, Georgia and sent to a military prison in Louisville, Kentucky on June 22, 1864. From there, he was sent to Rock Island Prison in Illinois and released from Rock Island Prison on June 20, 1865, at the age of 39.

I have some letters written during the Civil War by my ancestors that gave me insights into their lives. The story is fictional. The people were real, but I created the daily life. I hope you enjoy the book as you journey back into time.

Daniel Anderson Woodall
Warm Springs, Georgia
In his civil, war uniform
Confederate States of America

Chapter 1

Going To War

Daniel lifted his head from the pillow. Catherine was calling him, "Come home. Daniel, it's suppertime." She was framed against the blue sky, her dark hair blowing in the soft breeze.

Slowly, Daniel opened his eyes. He lay on a low hospital cot, all around him lay confederate soldiers—some dying, others recovering. Daniel knew he had been here a long time. He couldn't remember for sure how long. He did remember that he left Camp in Alabama in September. Then he remembered Chickamauga.

Closing his eyes, Daniel saw again the picture of Catherine. She kept him living each day. The hope of returning home to her and Baby Joey made him fight to stay alive. Some day this awful war would be over.

The day Daniel left Catherine floated through his mind. Joey had gone to stay with his parents. They had walked hand in hand through the cotton fields crossing the little branch into the woods. They sat on a mossy knoll under a beech tree. Their names were carved into the tree inside a small heart. Daniel had carved it there when they were sweethearts. Agonizing pain ran through Daniel with each beat of his heart. Leaving Catherine was the hardest thing he had ever done.

Catherine's eyes had searched his, her pain as apparent as his own. She would be left alone on the farm with a 10-month-old baby. Daniel's parents were near, but they had their own farm to care for. God gave Catherine the strength to tell Daniel it would be alright for him to go. They held each other, and then slowly returned home to prepare for Daniel's departure to war.

Daniel had saddled his horse with a great weight bearing down on his heart. He really was going. Catherine was preparing food in the kitchen. He would pick up the food, hold her close and be on his way.

Catherine lifted her face for Daniel's good-bye kiss. Her lips, sweet and warm, lingered on his. She did not cry, nor betray the awful turmoil in her heart. Daniel had been ordered to go. She would not make it harder for him.

Riding away, Daniel turned and lifted his hand. She waved good-bye, in the early morning sunlight, with a smile on her lips and tears streaming down her cheeks. The picture was stamped in Daniel's mind. He would treasure it until he returned.

A few miles down the road, Daniel was joined by other men. Their faces were as sober and sad as Daniel's, because they, too, had left loved ones behind. Thoughts of his parents and his son, who slept there, crossed his mind as he rode past the road that led to their home. Daniel had gone yesterday and said his "Good-byes." It had been so hard for Mama. Charlie and James, his younger brothers, had seemed confused that now Daniel must go. Rachel, his only sister, had sobbed as she kissed him good-bye. They were so close and had always shared everything in their lives. Rachel loved Catherine like a sister and promised Daniel she would help her with Joey. As Daniel held Rachel close, he thought, "She is so fragile." As always, Papa encouraged him to be brave and trust God to care for him. Daniel knew in his heart that their prayers would surround him daily.

Thoughts of war surfaced in Daniel's mind. "How do you kill another person?" What would he do when that time came? He had no enemies up until now, but the union army would be his enemy. They were coming to destroy a way of life he had always known. He owned no slaves and had no desire to do so, but he had been called to defend his country. He would fight until the end. He wondered how far from Warm Springs, Georgia, he would travel.

The soft, crusty bread Daniel pulled from his saddlebag smelled good. As he ate the bread, he realized it was the last of Catherine's cooking he would eat for a long time. He could see her small hands kneading the dough and shaping it into loaves. Some of Catherine's strength flowed into him as he ate and his spirits lifted; he believed God would watch over him and he would return to Catherine and Joseph.

Tired and sleepy, Daniel and his companions rode on through the night, before dawn they would arrive at Camp Quito.

"Daniel Anderson Woodall" a sharp, loud voice awakened Daniel as he jerked awake from a short sleep. "Come with me" the man in a gray uniform said.

Jumping to his feet, Daniel followed the soldier.

"Get in line here, you will be issued a uniform and a gun. Then you will sign papers and be part of the Confederate Army. You will be going to Camp Eufala in Alabama," he said.

The early morning sun rose warm and bright on this 28th day of March, 1863. Daniel stood quiet, moving with the line. He observed the man behind him. He moved along with a far away look in his eyes. Daniel didn't interrupt his thoughts.

The young man in front of Daniel talked and laughed with the man in front of him. He looked different than most of the men. His olive skin and black curly hair made Daniel wonder where his home was. His black eyes flashed when he laughed, and he spoke with a strange accent. He turned and stuck out his hand toward Daniel.

"Hello," he said, "I'm Garth Beley from South Louisiana."

Daniel grasped Garth's hand, feeling the steel grip upon his own. He knew whatever Garth had done before this, he had great strength.

A gray uniform and a gun were handed to Daniel. He signed the paper in front of him and walked away. He looked at the paper and read.

"Daniel Anderson Woodall
Muster Roll of Company B, 32nd Regiment
Georgia Volunteer Infantry
Army of Tennessee
Confederate States of America
Talbot County, Georgia"

Daniel's eyes lingered on the word volunteer.

Men continued to arrive at Camp Quito all through the day. By late afternoon, over a hundred men were mounted on their horses moving out to Camp Eufala. They were led by a young officer not much older than Daniel. Tomorrow, March 29th, Daniel would be 25 years old. It would be a hard day for Catherine. Perhaps she would bake a cake and she and Joey would sing "Happy Birthday." Daniel pictured them gathered around the table singing with her brown eyes sparkling, but Daniel knew in his heart it would not be like that. Catherine would weep when she was alone. She was only 20 years old and alone with a baby. Daniel's heart ached as he rode in formation with the soldiers.

There was much activity in Camp Eufala, soldiers coming and going in all directions. Daniel wondered how he would fit into this place.

A sergeant greeted the new recruits from Quito. "Put your horses in the corral and report to me in front of the camp kitchen in one hour," he ordered. "You will be assigned a tent and a bunk mate." Daniel put his horse in the corral and leaned against the fence, never had he felt so alone.

The sergeant began to call names and tent numbers. Daniel heard his name called along with Garth Beley, assigned to Tent 7. Moving through the men, Daniel found Garth.

"Looks like we will get to know each other real well," Garth said grinning.

Garth and Daniel moved away from the soldiers and walked toward a large meadow stretching to a pine forest beyond. Hundreds of tents covered the meadow, most of which were already occupied. Tent 7 was in the first row of tents next to the forest.

"Guess this will be home for a while," Garth said as he dropped his belongings on his bedroll.

Turning to Daniel, he asked, "What did you leave behind?"

Daniel looked into Garth's dark eyes and saw strength and honesty. He decided he could trust this man with the steel handshake.

"I left behind my heart, Garth. Years ago, I gave it to a girl named Catherine. We now own a farm and have a little boy named Joseph in Warm Springs, Georgia."

"It must have been awful, leaving I mean," Garth answered.

"Yes, it was," Daniel replied. "What did you leave behind, Garth?"

"Not nearly as much as you. No wife, no child, just my mama and papa and brothers and sister in the Bayou Country of Louisiana. I left there three years ago because I wanted to travel. I liked the people of Georgia, so I decided to join the men in my town and chase this union army back home."

"Did your family own slaves?" Daniel asked.

Throwing back his head, Garth laughed loudly. "No, Daniel, there were no slaves in my family. Just us Cajun Beleys working and fighting to make a living. We made boats to sell and wrestled alligators for fun."

"Wrestled alligators!" Daniel exclaimed, surprised.

"Yep, you can win every time if you get the right hold on them," Garth replied.

Now Daniel knew why Garth's grip was so strong.

Daniel's stomach was empty and aching.

"Come on, Garth," Daniel said, "Let's see what that kitchen is serving for supper, we need nourishment if we're going to learn how to fight a war."

Chapter 2

A Letter From Catherine

Tired and hungry, Daniel moved slowly through the chow line. The sergeant called for attention and all eyes turned toward him.

"Just wanted to tell you soldiers that a mail bag arrived today. 6:00 p.m. sharp we will have mail call," he said.

Excitement ran through the troops. Most of them had not heard from their families since they left home in March. Everyone hoped for a letter.

Daniel stood near the sergeant as he sorted through the letters and called out names. His hopes were high that he would receive a letter from Catherine. As the soldiers were handed their letters, Daniel's heart pounded as he waited. The sergeant was almost finished when he called Daniel's name.

A letter from Catherine, Daniel pressed it against his face. He could smell the faint lavender scent of his beloved.

Daniel dropped to his bedroll and opened his letter.

May 10, 1863

My Dearest Daniel,

I pray God will direct my letter to you.

Joey is growing. He eats almost everything, now that he has 10 teeth.

James Henry has come to live here with Joey and me. Mama and Papa made that decision. I am so thankful for their kindness in sending him. He is so much help on the farm and, at age 15, he is able to do a grown man's work. Your Papa taught him well. Joey loves him so much and follows him all over when he is in the house.

Oh, Daniel, it is so hard to tell you, but I must. Your Papa was called to war also; right after he had sent James to live here he received word that he must go. Mama insisted that she had Rachel and Charlie to help her and that James would stay here. Charlie is a great help, though he is only twelve.

Mama thinks that Papa is in Atlanta. Perhaps your paths might cross, but I pray you aren't sent to Atlanta, we hear there is heavy fighting. The union army would like to control the railroads that run through the city.

Do you know when you will go to battle? I know your training must be almost over and I have great difficulty thinking about what will come next. I pray God will place a shield around you and bring you safely home to Joey and me.

We missed you so much on your birthday. James, Joey and I sang "Happy Birthday" to you. We will celebrate when you return.

Bossy's calf was born three days after your birthday. We named her Dannybelle after you. She is a beautiful calf and should make a fine milk cow, like her mother. Some day, we will have a whole herd of cows.

The nights are the hardest, Daniel, when I am alone and all is quiet—it is so hard. God always hears my prayers and brings peace to my heart. I go to sleep holding you in my dreams.

The time is late, Daniel, and I get up before dawn, so I must close. I hope to receive a letter before you leave Camp Eufala. God be with you, my love.

Your loving wife,
Catherine

Folding his arms around his knees, Daniel rocked back and forth. His pain was intense. He missed Catherine so much; she was so brave and strong. Tomorrow he would write to her, soon he would be leaving Eufala and he didn't know what would come after that.

Daniel swatted the mosquitoes biting his neck and rolled over on his bedroll. He was hot with fever. He felt so weak and wondered what he should do. He knew he was sick, but at 4:30 a.m. he must rise for another day of training.

"Come on, Daniel," Garth yelled. "We have to reach the forest or we're dead."

The burning rays of the July sun blinded Daniel as he ran for cover and the end of his training drew near.

Daniel hurried away from supper. He wanted to write to Catherine before dark. Garth sat propped on his bedroll drawing. God had given Garth a great talent. He could draw pictures of animals that seemed alive. After greeting Garth, Daniel turned to his writing:

July 22, 1863

My Dearest Catherine,

I was so sure I would receive a letter when mail arrived yesterday. Your letter was wonderful.

Joey must be growing so fast. He had only four teeth when I left and now he has 10. Kiss him for me and tell him about his Papa, so he doesn't forget me.

*My dear, I must tell you that we will leave in September. I think
we are going to Charleston, South Carolina. It seems like we will most
likely ride on a train, if the Yankees don't blow up the tracks before
we can leave.*

*I wish I could have come home before we leave, but that will
not be possible. I don't have any idea when, if ever, I can come. Only
God knows, but I firmly hope and trust in Him that He will spare me
to come home sometimes; and I hope He will spare us all to meet on
earth again. It is all with God and His will must be done. I believe I
will come home to you and Joey.*

*I don't know if you will ever receive this letter, but I want you to
answer soon if you do. You must direct you letters to D. A. Woodall,
Co. B 32, Regt. Georgia Volunteer, Charleston, S.C. I have told them
here at Eufala if any letters come here for me after I am gone, to send
them back to Quito until I know for sure where I will be.*

*Give my love to all the family. I must say farewell to you, my lovely
wife and little babe so dear. God be with you.*

All my love,
Daniel (part of an original letter written by Daniel)

Daniel folded his letter and slowly addressed it.

Garth tore a page from his drawing pad, "This is for Catherine, please enclose it in your letter," he said.

Daniel looked at the picture. It was him, he felt like he was looking into a mirror.

"Thank you, Garth, Catherine will be so happy to have it," Daniel answered, with a faraway look in his clear blue eyes.

When the wake up bugle sounded at 4:30, Daniel rolled over and sat up. He felt dizzy and sick; pulling on his uniform, he wondered how he could go. He prayed to God for strength to train another day.

The sergeant called out at breakfast, "The captain wants all soldiers to report to his quarters at 6:00 a.m."

The soldiers stood waiting; when the captain appeared, they all snapped to attention and saluted. A strange quiet fell over the Regiment.

"At ease, men. I have received your orders," the captain announced. "You will all leave tomorrow at 5:00 a.m., if the train runs on time. You are going to Charleston, South Carolina. If you encounter the union army on your way, be prepared to go to battle. There will be no training today. Prepare for your journey, and God bless you all."

Garth reached out and gripped Daniel's shoulder as they walked quietly, side by side.

Chapter 3

The Yankees are Coming

Catherine peered from the doorway of the barn. Dark clouds overhead threatened rain. She turned and lifted Joey to her hip; if she hurried, maybe she could reach the house before the rain came.

Moving quickly with the milk pail and Joey, Catherine reached the porch. Out of the corner of her eye she caught a glimpse of a horseback rider coming down the road. Who would be coming so early in the morning and why would they be riding at such a break-neck speed? The rider came closer and Catherine recognized Daniel's sister. Something awful must have happened for Rachel to ride so fast.

Holding Joey tight, Catherine raced to meet Rachel.

Rachel's face was drawn and white as she jumped from the horse.

"What's wrong?" Catherine cried.

"The Yankees are coming. Mama sent me to warn you. Hide all the food you can. Hide Bossy and Dannybelle in the deep woods. They are taking the cows for meat," Rachel gasped.

Swinging back into the saddle, Rachel left swiftly to warn the neighbors.

Catherine sprang into action. Without Bossy, there would be no milk for Joey.

Yelling for James, she rushed to the barn. Placing Joey in the tall feed box, she grabbed a rope and tied it around Bossy and the calf. Thank God James had taken the wagon and the horses to Mama's yesterday. She hoped Mama was able to hide them.

James appeared panting and white faced. "What's wrong?" he cried.

"The Yankees are coming, they are gathering food for their army." Pressing the lead ropes into his hand, she cried, "Hide the cow and calf in the woods behind the beech tree."

James grabbed a sharp hatchet and more rope and hurried from the barn.

Catherine's next thought was the laying hens and where they would be feeding this time of day. She hoped they were in the edge of the woods out of sight.

Picking up a basket, Catherine hurried from the barn with Joey. The baby clung tightly to her, sensing something was dreadfully wrong. Near the pear tree, she sat Joey down and shook the tree furiously. Pears covered the ground as she continued to shake. Filling the basket, she buried it in the hayloft.

Racing back to the house, Joey was laid in his bed. The morning milk still sat on the porch. Catherine strained it and hid it behind her bed. She washed the milk pail and put it away.

Her next thought was of the corn meal James had brought home from the mill yesterday. Where could she hide it? Dumping the stove wood, she placed two 25-pound bags in the bottom of the box and arranged the wood on top. The other two bags, she left in the cupboard.

Returning to Joey's room, Catherine looked in and found him sound asleep. Slowly, she sank into the rocking chair and stared at her baby, breathing a prayer to ask God to keep them safe. In the distance, she heard horses approaching and knew that the union soldiers would soon be at her door.

A heavy knock sounded through the house. Catherine arose and went to the door. Opening the door, she looked out at a young union officer.

"We need food, Ma'am. We will be gathering things from your farm," he said. Catherine nodded.

The officer entered the kitchen door and went to the pantry.

"Are you alone?"

"No, my little boy is sleeping in the next room."

Turning, he went to Joey's door and looked down upon the sleeping child.

"Where is his father?" the soldier asked.

"Gone to war," Catherine replied.

"He is a beautiful child." Catherine nodded again.

Returning to the pantry, he picked up one of the bags of corn meal and left the kitchen.

Several soldiers came around the house. They carried all the late fall collard greens and all the pears left on the pear tree.

"Anything you want us to put in the wagon from the house?" a soldier asked.

The officer handed the bag of corn meal to him.

"There are two fat pigs in a pen behind the barn. Shall we shoot them and take them along?"

Catherine's heart sank; she had forgotten the pigs that would be butchered for their winter meat.

"Take only one," the officer said. His glance fell upon Catherine as she stood in the doorway.

Her eyes met the young soldiers and she nodded her head and whispered, "Thank you." Kindness, she thought, in a union soldier. Truly God had answered her prayers.

Catherine winced as a shot rang out. Two soldiers came around the barn carrying the pig. She was grateful they had left one for winter food.

The officer moved from the porch. Tipping his head in her direction, he said "Good Day, Madam."

As the soldiers left her yard, Catherine prayed for her neighbors.

Hearing Joey's cry, Catherine turned and entered the house with trembling knees. Going to the crib, she lifted Joey and sank into the rocking chair.

I must find James, Catherine thought, as she rose from the chair.

James loaded baskets of sweet potatoes into the wagon. There was not much food to harvest after the sweep the union army had made in their community. The northern soldiers did not know the sweet potatoes were under the ground and had passed them by. The sweet potato crop had been spared, and he was grateful.

Today, James would trade potatoes for other food, and go to the post office.

Returning to the house, James bid Catherine good-bye and swung Joey up into his arms for a good-bye kiss.

"Go," Joey squealed.

"No, you can't go today. I'm not going to see Grandma. Maybe tomorrow you can go," James said.

Joey played under the kitchen table while Catherine peeled and sliced sweet potatoes to dry. Combined and ground with parched rye, the dried potatoes made a hot drink that everyone was calling confederate coffee. Catherine hoped James could trade potatoes for a bag of rye grain.

In Warm Springs, James was able to trade the sweet potatoes for the supplies they needed.

He stopped at the General Store and Post Office on his way home. There wasn't likely to be any mail, but he had promised Catherine he would stop.

"Hello, Mr. Blagg, any mail for us Woodalls?" James called.

"Oh, yes, James. I'm glad you asked. There is a letter for Catherine and it's from Daniel."

Slapping the horses with the reins, James hurried home.

Pulling the wagon beside the porch, James unloaded all the supplies and called to Catherine. He handed her the letter.

Clutching the letter to her breast, Catherine said, "Supper is almost ready. I will read the letter after supper."

Catherine set the table with trembling hands and James blessed their food.

"Come on, Joey, let's walk to the branch. Maybe we will see some fish, and your mama can have some quiet while she reads her letter," James said.

Catherine nodded her head and smiled her thanks, as she pulled the rocking chair near the window. The late afternoon sunlight streamed into the room and bathed her in a golden light as she opened Daniel's letter.

A single piece of paper fell from the letter. Catherine unfolded it and Daniel stared out at her. With a cry, she held it to her face and cried, "My Beloved."

Every fiber and nerve in Catherine's body ached as she read Daniel's letter and knew that he had gone to war. She sat sobbing in the golden light.

Chapter 4

War and Sickness

The rising sun cast a red glow in the eastern sky as Daniel's regiment milled around waiting for the train. In the distance, the sound of the steam engine whistle drifted across the countryside. Daniel shivered in the coolness of the early morning. Sometimes he was so hot. Other times cold chills gripped his body and he shook uncontrollably. He knew he was sick, but he must continue on until this war was over.

The shuddering train pulled into the station. Daniel, Garth and all the regiment climbed aboard the train.

Garth grinned at Daniel and said, "It won't be as bad as training a wild horse."

The train gathered speed and soon Camp was a speck on the horizon.

They were going to Atlanta and their orders said from Atlanta to Charleston, South Carolina; however, if they encountered the union army, they would stop and fight.

Early the following day, the train pulled into the Atlanta Railway Station. An army officer stood waiting to give their commander orders. The orders came, swift and brief. All the soldiers would be sent to fight the union army at Chickamauga Creek. The creek divided Tennessee and Georgia.

General Braxton Bragg was leading the confederate troops against Major General William Rosecrans. Daniel listened carefully as all the soldiers were briefed on what would be coming. They would leave Atlanta tonight.

Daniel's thoughts were on his father. Could he find him in this war-torn city, in the few hours he would be here? How he longed to see his gentle face and feel his warm embrace.

"Come on, Daniel, it's time to eat," Garth called. Moving away from the station, Daniel's eyes scanned every passing face. Questions ran through Daniel's mind. Who could he ask where he might find Papa? Following Garth, he moved through the streets to the army mess hall.

A tall man hurried toward the train station. He dodged around the soldiers. Daniel stopped dead in his tracks. The man looked older and had grown a beard, but it was Papa.

"Papa!" Daniel cried.

The man heard the voice and rushed forward running to meet Daniel with outstretched arms.

"My son, my son!" he cried with tears streaming down his face.

"Oh, Papa, it is so good to see you again."

"I heard a regiment was being sent from Camp Eufala. I thought you might be with them, so I came as soon as I finished my morning duties hoping I might find you."

"You look so tired, Papa. Has your company been through lots of fighting?"

"Yes, the union army would sure like to control Atlanta. We have fought hard and many have died."

"Can you come with us now?" Daniel asked.

"Yes," replied Papa, "I am off duty until 6:00 p.m."

"We leave at 5:00 for Chickamauga."

"I know, son, General Hood briefed us."

"Garth, this is my father, Captain William Woodall," Daniel said.

Garth saluted the captain.

"At ease, son, now we are just father and son and friend."

"I know you are a good man, sir, because you have raised your son up to be a fine man," Garth replied.

Daniel smiled, thinking how blessed he was to have found a friend like Garth.

The afternoon passed swiftly as Daniel, Garth and Papa talked. At 4:00 p.m., all the soldiers returned to the train station. A sober mood fell upon the soldiers as they approached the train.

Turning to Papa, Daniel gathered him in his arms and bid him farewell.

"God be with you, Daniel, and you, too, Garth!" Papa said.

As the train pulled away, Daniel's eyes followed Papa. He raised his arm and saluted. With tears in his eyes, he wondered if he would ever see Papa again.

The harvest moon rose over the trees. Bright yellow, it lit the countryside. This same moon would be shining on Warm Springs. Daniel remembered how he used to wake in the night and watch Catherine sleeping in the moonlight. Now he moved through his home, he watched his beloved sleeping and Joey tumbling about in his crib. James would be sleeping in the small room behind the kitchen. Tears gathered in his eyes. Good night, dear family, he whispered.

Daniel's last thoughts were of Papa, guarding Atlanta, as he drifted off to sleep.

The train came to a clanging halt in the little town of Dalton. There was no activity in the early morning light. The General Store was not open, but a confederate captain came to direct them to a training post nearby.

The sun rose warming the early fall morning. A gentle breeze rustled the leaves on the tall oak trees as Daniel and the regiment marched to Dalton training center, passing the church, school and community center. Daniel was cold and shook with a chill, as he so often did.

Garth watched his friend and worried about him. He had urged Daniel to see the army doctor before they left Eufala, but Daniel always though he would get better. Today, he was so weak he could hardly stand. Finding a place in a sunny spot, Garth left Daniel in search of breakfast.

Daniel sat alone, his head resting on his hands. Suddenly he raised his head, someone was watching him. He looked straight into the startling blue eyes of a tall man about Papa's age.

"What's wrong, son? You don't look so good," the stranger said.

"No, sir, I'm pretty sick," Daniel said.

"Did you just arrive on the train?"

"Yes," Daniel answered.

"I'm Stuart Harmon from Louisiana," the man said. "Let me get you something hot to drink."

"Thank you," Daniel replied. "I'm Daniel Woodall from Georgia and I could sure use a hot drink."

The man walked away quickly and soon returned with a tin cup of hot liquid. "Confederate coffee," he said, "but it's not bad when you get used to the taste."

As the warmth of the hot liquid seeped into Daniel, he began to feel better.

Stuart seated himself across from Daniel. "I arrived yesterday from Atlanta," he said. "Guess we will all cross Chickamauga Creek tomorrow at day break. Big battle brewing with this General Rosecrans and all his union army."

"Yes," answered Daniel.

"I'm a little worried about this battle, Daniel. So many soldiers arriving, must be a big one. I don't mind dying so much, but I sure hate to leave my dear wife, Grace, and young son, Matthew. If God sees fit to take me home to heaven, I know He will care for my loved ones. I'm sure lonesome for them today, maybe I'll write a letter and hope somehow to get it mailed," Stuart said.

Stuart leaned against the tree trunk and closed his eyes. Daniel shivered; he didn't know if it was another chill or fear.

Garth returned, bringing Daniel a tin cup of hot corn meal mush.

"Thanks, Garth, for looking after me. Meet Stuart Harmon, he arrived yesterday from Atlanta, but he's from your state."

Stuart stood up and shook Garth's hand. "Nice to meet you, Garth, I'll leave Daniel in your care now," he said. "I'll probably see you tomorrow."

A quiet mood settled over Dalton. The soldiers strolled around talking and waiting, many wrote letters home. The late afternoon sun was warm on this 18th day of September 1863.

Daniel slept and rested most of the day. Thoughts of Catherine came so strong, and he remembered a promise he had made to her. Someday, I will build you a stone flowerbed in the front yard. He had never had the time, now he silently vowed if he ever returned home he would build the flowerbed.

Before dawn, every soldier was ready to cross Chickamauga Creek. Many soldiers had been issued horses and the Calvary would go first.

Garth and Daniel were foot soldiers and they would march behind the Calvary. All the confederate soldiers were under the command of General Braxton Bragg, who had been joined by James Longstreet who brought his army from Virginia. Twelve thousand men had arrived by train last night from Atlanta. A sooty train would be remembered for the extraordinary transporting of so many soldiers to one battle.

Red and purple streaks spread across the eastern sky as the first rays of the rising sun touched the horizon. In the distance the sound of a bugle rang out, the union army was moving.

The Calvary passed through the shallow muddy waters of the Chickamauga. Daniel and Garth moved forward pressed on each side by other soldiers, up a little knoll and out into a large open meadow.

As the sun rose, cannonballs began to explode. Horses screamed and officers yelled orders. Men were running and firing. Garth was sent one direction. Daniel stood alone, frozen to the ground. "Oh, God, what should I do," Daniel prayed. Then he clearly heard the command "Forward with Courage, Daniel."

Daniel ran, firing his gun. He stumbled over the feet of a dead soldier. He looked down into the blank blue eyes of Stuart Harman and remembered Stuart's words, "If God chooses to take me, He will take care of my loved ones." Catherine's face floated through Daniel's mind.

The battle raged on all day; when night fell, dead and wounded soldiers covered the meadow. Daniel shook with exhaustion and fear as they retreated across Chickamauga. He searched for Garth as soldiers milled around him.

Too sick to eat the meager rations offered to him, Daniel fell into an exhausted sleep in the woods near the creek. His weary mind searched for Garth even in his sleep.

Exploding cannonballs whined overhead as the union army approached the creek bed. The confederate army, tattered and much smaller than yesterday, rose up to fight a second day.

A slow, steady rain beaded and ran off Daniel's uniform; the Georgia countryside was misty and dark as the soaking rain continued. The foot soldiers moved across the creek. Their battle cry was, "Send Rosecrans back to Chattanooga." The fighting was desperate, but Longstreet and his men broke through the union line and sent it reeling and, indeed, they did send Rosecrans back to Chattanooga.

A victory cry rose up from the confederate soldiers. Daniel looked across the meadow at the human carnage and fell face down as blackness enveloped him.

Chapter 5

The Makeshift Hospital

Two medics approached Daniel's still body and rolled him over.

"Is he dead?" one asked.

"I don't know, he doesn't seem to be shot," the other answered.

"He's not dead, his skin is hot and he has a faint heartbeat, better load him into the wagon going to the hospital. Wonder what's wrong with him," the first medic said.

The medics continued across the meadow looking for wounded soldiers. Thousands lay dead and would be picked up by others and buried.

"General says we won the battle," one medic said, "but you wonder if it was worth what it cost us with so many wounded and dead."

The medics' wagon moved slowly, pulled by two stout mules. Daniel's body bounced as they drove over the rough ground. Daniel was locked inside the darkness. He never felt the sticky blood that ran into the bottom of the wagon and stained his uniform, as the lifeblood of his companion soldier drained into the wagon.

"This one's sick. I thought he was shot from all the blood on his uniform, but the blood must have come from this poor fellow whose leg was almost shot off," the surgeon said. "Put this sick soldier in a room alone until we find out why he has such a high fever."

Daniel was placed on a stretcher and carried to a main washroom, where his uniform was removed and he was bathed. Then he was place in isolation in a small room. Doctors came and treated him; they decided he had a terrible case of malaria. He would be treated with the medicine the Spanish missionaries in South America had discovered in 1630, quinine made from the bark of the cinchona tree.

Each day, the women who volunteered to feed the soldiers came to Daniel and slowly fed him hot broth. He was moved from the small room into the main ward.

Daniel was awake and all the terrible memories of Chickamauga came flooding into his mind. Garth, what happened to Garth? Poor Stuart Harmon, he remembered that Stuart had died, he prayed for Grace and her son, Matthew. The awful sound of battle echoed through Daniel's mind as he drifted in and out of consciousness. He clung to the dream of Catherine; it made him want to live.

A medic appeared with an older woman. "Hello, Daniel, meet Sarah Whisler," he said. "She volunteers and helps us take care of all you guys. She took great care of you while you were out of things."

Sarah moved to Daniel's side. "Hello, Daniel, I'm so glad to see you are awake," she said. She smiled the sweetest smile and took Daniel's hand. "I prayed many prayers for you as I spooned hot broth into you."

Daniel gazed up at the woman; she was tall and slender with a stately look about her. "Why had she cared about him?" he wondered. He soon learned why.

Sarah loved God and because of her love of God she gave each day to caring for the soldiers brought to this makeshift hospital in the Community Center of Dalton. Truly, they had all become her brothers.

"Thank you, Sarah, for all your care," Daniel whispered.

Daniel looked around the ward. He counted the beds, two rows, and eight beds in each row. Sixteen men waiting to be well so they could return to the war. Some would never return to the battlefield—arms, legs, hands and feet were missing.

Tears slid down Daniels cheeks as he looked at the men, closing his eyes he wanted to go back into the darkness where there was no war and pain. He knew he could not live in the darkness, so tomorrow he would try to stand and be someone's hand or leg.

Calling out a cheery "Good Morning," Sarah arrived with breakfast. Daniel accepted his bowl and said to Sarah, "Today I will stand and walk, and tomorrow I will help you."

"That's wonderful," Sarah replied. "We could sure use another pair of hands around here. Perhaps you could sit and make Lambs' ears bandages. Daniel didn't know what lamb's ear bandages were, but if Sarah needed them he would learn to make them.

The next day, Sarah arrived carrying a large basket filled with silvery soft leaves.

"This is Lambs' ears, Daniel. It is an herb that helps wounds to heal. We have used so much of it in this war that it is becoming scarce. You can sew it together almost like cloth."

Pushing the needle through the soft leaf, Daniel settled in to making his first bandage. Leaf after leaf was sewed together making a long strip, which would be wrapped around a leg or arm.

After a busy morning, Daniel felt weak and tired. "Enough, Daniel," Sarah said as she took the basket away. "You must rest now."

The days passed slowly, Daniel couldn't understand why he was so weak. Today, he would ask Dr. Harris why he could not gain his strength back.

When Dr. Harris reached Daniel's cot, he asked if he could talk to him about his illness.

"You have a very serious illness. Malaria, when left untreated for a long time as yours was, has caused liver damage and you are very anemic. You are still running a fever and having chills. We hope the quinine will kill the parasites in your blood and slowly the chills and fevers will disappear, but it will take weeks," the doctor said.

A deep sadness settled over Daniel. In his mind he wondered, "Will I ever be well again, will I ever go home to Catherine and Joey?"

October leaves began to fall. Sarah encouraged Daniel to write to Catherine and let her know where he was. He hesitated to write because he didn't want Catherine to know how sick he was.

Bringing paper and pencil, Sarah said, "Write, Daniel! Catherine will be happy to know you are alive. I'm sure by now the news of Chickamauga has spread back to Warm Springs."

Pulling himself up, Daniel clutched his bed waiting for the dizziness to pass. Taking his blanket, he moved from the ward to a small visitors room that was quiet and sunny. Slipping into a chair that sat in the sun, he settled to write to Catherine.

October 20, 1863

My Dearest Catherine,

It is hard to write when I have no good news, but I guess being alive is good news when so many died.

The Battle of Chickamauga was so awful, thousands died on both sides.

I was found unconscious on the battlefield and brought to Dalton to this Community Center, which has been turned into a makeshift hospital. I have malaria, I have been very sick but I am getting better. Many of the soldiers have lost hands and arms and legs and feet.

My dizzy spells, chills and fevers are all improving. I try to do everything I can to help in the ward, but I'm afraid I'm not much help.

So often I wonder how long this war will last and how many must die before we stop this madness, surely we can learn to live in peace without slaves. All people should be free to work and live and have a happy family no matter the color of our skin.

I have much time to pray and I remember all of you. I always pray you are safe and that you have food. There are so many concerns, but I am learning to trust all things into God's hands.

Papa and I spent several hours together in Atlanta. It was a blessed gift from God to see him. He looked older and so tired, and he has grown a beard. I don't know if he knows I am alive or not. He knew I was going to Chickamauga.

*Garth and I were separated during the battle. I have no way of
knowing if he is still out there fighting or if he died at Chickamauga.
I pray he survived the battle and went on to Charleston as were our
original orders, perhaps someday we will meet again.*

*Beloved, I am so weary. I must close and return to my bed to sleep.
I hope and pray I will soon be stronger.*

*Write to me in care of Dalton Community Center Hospital. A dear
woman named Sarah, who cared for me when I was unconscious, said
she would mail this for me.*

*Always I see you in my dreams and I cling to that. Kiss Joey and
tell him about his Papa. Give Mama and the family my love. Until we
meet again, God be with you.*

*Love always,
Daniel*

Picking up his blanket and letter, Daniel walked slowly holding on to the wall. He wondered why he was so weak.

The night sounds of the ward flowed around Daniel. Jeb tossed in his cot, next to him. Jeb's leg had been blown off at Chickamauga. He was having a difficult time accepting the fact that his leg was gone. He lay in deep depression when awake and seldom talked to anyone. The wound was not healing and often the bandages were bloody, the doctors were fighting infection and Jeb's life hung in the balance. A low moan escaped his lips as he slept.

All the bright fall leaves turned brown and drifted to the ground, leaving the trees stark and bare. Cold rains came often and Thanksgiving drew near.

Dr. Harris arrived early on a dark, dreary morning. "Hey, you guys better spruce up this ward, because someone special is coming for a visit," he called out.

All the men looked up waiting to hear who was coming.

Jeb answered, "If it's Santa Claus, ask him to bring me a new leg." The men all laughed, they were happy Jeb was getting better and learning to accept his disability.

"No, not Santa Claus," the doctor replied. "It is General Robert E. Lee. Have any of you met him?"

No one in the ward had met the great confederate General.

"Well, fellows, you are in for a treat. I met him right after the war started. I heard him say if he owned 4,000,000 slaves, he would give them for the preservation of the union. He really didn't want this war to happen. President Lincoln wanted him to stand with the north, but he was a Virginian and came to stand with his own. The General is coming to Atlanta and he wants to ride the train to Dalton to greet all of you. Soon this hospital will be a Community Center again. Some of you will be transferred to the Atlanta Hospital, a few will be discharged and sent home and the rest of you will join the soldiers in Atlanta."

A deep quiet fell in the ward when the doctor left. Each man thought about the news and what it would mean to them.

Daniel thought of Catherine and Joey. He knew he would be returning to Atlanta to rejoin the army. He wondered if Catherine had received his letter and hoped he might hear from her before he left Dalton.

Jeb leaned his crutches against Daniel's bed and sat down. "Just want to thank you for all the prayers and encouragement you have given me since we woke up here side by side. At first, I really wanted to die. I couldn't see how I could make a living with only one leg, but you have shown me that God must have a plan for my life. I will look forward to going home to Mama and Papa. Someday I might find a girl who could love a one legged guy," he said.

Smiling, Daniel reached out and hugged his friend. "I'm sure you will have a good life," he said.

"I'm glad I will be going to Atlanta. My Papa is there serving under General Hood. I saw him for one afternoon before we were sent to Chickamauga. Maybe I can find him when I get there," Daniel said.

Thanksgiving Day dawned crisp with sunshine. The cold rains had passed and Indian summer came to the countryside.

The community of Dalton and the hospital staff had planned a great Thanksgiving dinner for the soldiers. Chicken and dressing, with mashed potatoes and gravy and sweet potato pie.

Daniel looked forward to dinner. He had not been able to eat for so long, but as his body healed his appetite returned.

Sarah came into the ward with their dinner, the aroma was wonderful. All the men bowed their heads as Sarah blessed their dinner. She thanked God for each man's life and asked His protection, as they would soon all be leaving Dalton.

General Lee came three days after Thanksgiving.

Daniel watched the General move through the ward. He warmly greeted each soldier, shaking hands. When he came to a man who had no arm or hand, he laid his hand on their shoulder thanking them for their sacrifice.

It was easy to see General Lee was a man with a gentle nature and a great devotion to his duty as leader of the confederate army. Daniel knew he had graduated from West Point in 1829, second in his class of 46. In spite of all the killing and dying, this man remained unbroken and unembittered. He was a symbol of courage for all the soldiers who served under him.

As the General approached his cot, Daniel stood. "Good morning, sir, thank you for coming to visit us," he said extending his hand.

"Thank you, soldier, for what you have given to your country," the General replied as he gripped Daniel's hand.

The General said, "God be with each of you," and he saluted the soldiers. The soldiers who were able rose and saluted the General as he left the ward.

The doctors and staff consulted with General Lee and the decision was made that Dalton Community Center Hospital would be closed December 1, 1863.

The last day in the ward passed slowly. Daniel and Jeb exchanged addresses. "Maybe someday, when the war is over, we might be able to visit. I will bring my beautiful wife and handsome children to see you," Jeb said laughing.

The sun was dim in the winter sky as Daniel watched the postman from the General Store bringing the mail.

Sarah appeared in the ward with three letters, one was for Daniel. His heart pounded as he tore open Catherine's letter.

Chapter 6

Picking the Cotton

A pink flush colored the eastern sky as dawn crept over the horizon.

James whistled softly and Catherine walked quietly. Today they would start picking the cotton. God had blessed their hard work of planting and chopping and now the harvest was ready, the long rows of white cotton stretched across the field to the woods.

Joey had stayed overnight with Rachel. She would care for him while Catherine and James harvested the crop. She would also make their evening meals. Everyone worked together to survive in this time of war. Rachel was unable to work in the fields, the hot sun made her sick and she vomited every time she was hot and overtired. Mama said old Dr. White had told her long ago that Rachel's heart was enlarged. Rachel did everything she could to help. Her disposition was sweet and gentle, and she loved Joey dearly.

Catherine stood straight, removing her hat so the slight breeze could cool her wet head. The sun had slipped behind a fluffy cloud giving a few moments of shade. Her back ached from the bent position and a vivid picture entered Catherine's mind. She remembered passing a large cotton plantation when she was a child. She had asked her mother, "Who are all those people picking the cotton?"

"They are slaves, dear, they belong to the plantation owner," Mother said.

"Who do the children belong to, Mother?" Catherine asked as she watched a young girl about her age pulling a heavy bag.

"The children belong to the slave owners also, Catherine," Mother answered.

Catherine asked no more questions, but the picture remained in her mind for a long time. She had decided then that children should not be slaves. Now Catherine knew that no one should be a slave. She felt the same feelings Daniel had expressed in his letter. All people should be free to live together in a family and work to earn their own living.

Dropping to her knees, Catherine returned to her picking, her mind in a turmoil. Daniel was fighting a war that should not be, if the South won slavery would continue and she knew slavery was wrong.

34

James emptied the heavy bags into the wagon. Catherine sat on the end of the wagon.

"You okay?" James asked.

"Yes, James, I'm bone weary tired, my hands are bleeding and my back feels like it will never stop aching, but I'm okay," Catherine said.

"It will be easier when your muscles adjust to all the bending," James replied.

James had picked cotton since he was ten years old. From age six to ten he had many jobs: he brought cool buckets of water to the hot field; he helped his mother gather vegetables from the garden and shelled peas and beans; at age 10, he went to the field with Papa and learned to pick cotton. Papa always told him what a fine job he did, picking fast and clean.

As the sun sank into the western sky, James called to Catherine, "Let's go to Mama's for supper."

The fall days passed quickly and at last the cotton crop was harvested.

Catherine slept along in the double bed, her dark hair spread over her face. She lay on Daniel's side of the bed, holding his pillow in her arms. When Daniel had first gone to war, she had muffled her sobs into the pillow. Now she held it near her, always with the thought, "Some day, Daniel will sleep beside me again."

The moonlight spilled across Catherine's bed; she sat upright, her dream still vivid in her mind. She had seen Daniel in a hospital bed and he had told her to go to the post office.

James was awake when Catherine entered the kitchen.

"You're up early," he called out.

"Oh, James, I couldn't stay in bed. I had a dream that seemed so real. Daniel was in a hospital bed and he told me to go to the post office. He is not dead, James, he's alive! I just know it!"

"We were so busy picking the cotton we forgot to go to the post office. Do you want me to go?" he asked.

"Thank you for offering, but I would like to go myself. Aren't you supposed to help Mama today?"

"Yes, I need to help Mama and Charlie finish picking their cotton before the fall rains," James said.

"I will ask Rachel to watch Joey when I take you to Mama's, then I will go to town and the post office. There are a few things I need from Mr. Blagg's General Store," Catherine said.

After breakfast, James went to the barn to milk Bossy and to hitch the horses to the wagon. Returning to the kitchen, he strained the milk and took it to the well, lowering the container into the cold water.

"Should I get you some money, Catherine?" James called from the kitchen.

"Yes, James, I will need one dollar," Catherine answered.

James carefully removed one board from the floor in his room; he had built a small wooden box under the floor to keep the money they had received for the three bales of cotton. It would have to last for a long time and they had agreed this was a safe place to keep the money.

The October sky looked like a cornflower blue bowl turned upside down as the wagon bounced along the gravel road.

Joey laughed and pointed at the noisy flock of crows feeding beside the road. The crows flapped away into the nearest sweet gum tree.

"Oh, Joey, look at the gum tree! Can you believe how red and purple the leaves have turned since we had frost!" Catherine exclaimed.

Catherine drank in the beauty of the fall day, wishing they had time to stop and gather some of the sticky gum that oozed from the gum tree. She and Joey often went to their woods and gathered the sweet gum to chew.

Leaving James and Joey at Mama's, Catherine hurried the horses toward town.

"Good morning, Mr. Blagg," she called to the storekeeper. "Is the post office open yet?"

"Yes, Catherine, the post office opens when I open the store and I'm so glad you finally came. I have had a letter for you for several days."

Catherine's eyes blurred with tears as she looked at the familiar handwriting.

"I'll be back to do some shopping later," Catherine said as she left the store.

Calling to the horses and tapping them lightly with the reins, Catherine hurried to the edge of town where someone had built a wooden bench under a giant oak tree.

Before opening the letter, Catherine thanked God that Daniel was alive. After the news of Chickamauga, she had faltered in her faith when she heard that over 2,000 had died. After days of intense prayer, Catherine felt at peace and her belief that Daniel was alive had returned.

Slowly Catherine unfolded the single page. Her face was wet with tears as she learned of the malaria, chills and fevers. So sick for so long but still alive, all in one piece and getting better.

Returning to the store, Catherine made her selections quickly. Ten cents for a hair ribbon for Rachel, she was so good to Joey, and the ribbon must be royal blue to match Rachel's good blue dress. Thirty cents for heavy flannel material to make James a shirt for Christmas. Ten cents for penny candy for Joey, Charlie and James to share. Twenty cents for a block of brown sugar, there was no sugar left in the kitchen sugar box. Five cents for buttons for James' shirt and twenty-five cents for a bag of flour.

Catherine waited while Mr. Blagg loaded her things in the wagon.

"How is Daniel doing?" he asked.

"He is in a hospital being treated for malaria, but he is getting better," Catherine replied.

The afternoon sun was warm as Catherine rode through the country. She allowed the horses to slow to a walk as she enjoyed the quiet time alone to pray and think about Daniel. She always closed her prayer with the thought, "Thank you, God, for bringing an end to this awful war and for bringing Daniel home."

Flapping the reins against the horses, she quickened their pace. The sun was dropping low and there were chores to be done before dark.

The tantalizing smell of baked yams and pork floated across the porch. As Catherine approached the kitchen door, she realized how hungry she was.

Mama opened the door, calling, "You're just in time for supper."

Handing the letter to Mama, Catherine said, "Go read Daniel's letter. I will help Rachel put supper on the table."

Joey, Charlie and James burst through the door laughing. "Boy, am I hungry!" James said.

Joey ran to Catherine, hugging her legs. "Eat," he said.

Mama returned from the porch and handed Catherine the letter. "Thank God he survived the battle and that he and Papa had an opportunity to be together. I know that they were both stronger because of that visit."

James blessed their meal and a quiet fell over the table as they ate.

Pushing his chair from the table, James said, "Mama, that Pork Roast was absolutely delicious. You need to teach Catherine to cook like that."

Catherine threw the towel she was wiping Joey's face with at James. He ducked, caught the towel and threw it back.

"You'd better mind your manners, boy, or there will be no candy for you," Catherine laughed as she produced the candy bag and passed it around the table.

"Rachel, this little gift is for you."

"Oh, Catherine, you shouldn't have," Rachel smiled her thanks and hugged her. "It will look great with my blue dress, maybe Jacob White will know I'm alive if I wear this to church on Sunday."

"Rachel, you know Jacob knows you are alive. He just hasn't been able to accept the fact that he has only one arm. Ever since he was sent home, he has struggled to accept himself," Catherine replied.

Catherine bathed Joey while James milked Bossy and fed the animals. Joey ran around the kitchen in his flour sack nightshirt. Before bed, Catherine always read to Joey from the Bible and showed him Daniel's picture.

Pulling the rocking chair near the lamp, Catherine lifted Joey into her lap. Opening the Bible, she removed Daniel's picture.

"Papa, Papa," Joey said.

"Yes, Joey, this is your Papa. He had to go away for a time, but you and I are waiting for him to return."

Kissing Joey's chubby cheek, Catherine placed him in his crib. "Good night, little man," she called as she left the room.

Catherine set the lamp on the small table beside her bed. Now she would write to Daniel.

November 15, 1863

My Dearest Daniel,

   I received your letter today, you came to me in a dream and told me to go to the post office. No one had been to town since September.

   James and I were so busy in September and October picking the cotton. We picked three bales and sold it at the gin. A buyer came from Atlanta and bought most of the local cotton. Mama sold three bales, also, and probably has two more. James and Charlie will finish her picking this week.

   Joey is growing and learning to talk. When I take your picture from the Bible, he calls you Papa. He will know you when you return.

   I am so glad you went to the Community Center Hospital so you could be treated for the malaria. You could have died if you hadn't received treatment. God does hear our prayers and watches over us.

   James is a blessing. He has done so much for us. I don't know how I could have managed without him. Today, I bought some warm flannel to make him a shirt for Christmas.

   I don't want to think of Christmas without you, Daniel. Remember our first Christmas together. Thank God for our memories. I cling to them, always thinking of the time when you return. Life will return to normal after this war is over.

   James is making a very special Christmas present for Joey. You know how James loves to whittle. He started whittling farm animals; so far he has made a cow, a horse and a pig. He has also made a log barn. He plans to have many more animals completed in time for Christmas.

   Mama was so happy to hear that you and Papa had spent an afternoon together. I hope you get to see him again when you leave Dalton. Tell him about James and Joey if you get to see him.

   Beloved, I must go. It is very late and Joey will be up at daybreak. The days are busy and thank God they are, not much time to dwell on sad thoughts.

   God be with you.

Love always,
Catherine

Chapter 7

Going Back to Atlanta

Daniel collected all the letters the men in the ward had written to Sarah. Sarah arrived with breakfast and Daniel gave her the letters.

Sarah said, "I am not going to cry because I am happy you are all going on with your lives."

"We will miss you, Sarah, and we thank you for your love and care," Daniel replied.

Smiling through her tears, Sarah said, "My prayers go with each of you. I was glad for the opportunity to come to this hospital and help care for all of you. You laid your life on the line to defend the confederacy. I pray this war will soon end and you will all go home to your families."

The train whistle sounded mournful in the distance. Daniel and Jeb stood waiting to board the train with all the soldiers from the hospital.

Sarah had fixed the leg of Jeb's uniform so he could manage with his good leg and crutches.

"Good-bye, Jeb," Daniel said as he hugged his friend. They stood watching all the seriously wounded soldiers being transferred to the Atlanta Hospital.

Jeb waved as the train moved out, Daniel waved and turned away with the soldiers returning to war. A soldier waited for the men arriving from Dalton, "You will be joining Company C here in Atlanta. We will notify your company that you have recovered and are being transferred to this company."

Following the soldiers to the barracks, Daniel's thoughts turned to Papa. Somewhere in Atlanta, he hoped to find him.

Daniel asked his sergeant, "Do you know Captain William Woodall?"

"No," the sergeant replied, "but I haven't been here very long. When the captain of our unit returns, ask him."

Dusk fell early; a chilly wind was blowing as Daniel and the other soldiers arrived at the barracks. Daniel shivered, the chills and fever still came at times. The doctor had given him all the quinine he had left at the Dalton Hospital. He had told Daniel to take a dose every day until it was gone.

Daniel and his unit were now under the command of General Hood.

Atlanta was a vital town for the Confederacy, connected to the southern states by the Atlantic Railroad. Atlanta's manufacturing and storage of supplies made it a city the union army would like to control. The railroad was the reason a large army hospital was located in Atlanta. Wounded soldiers arrived daily.

Daniel liked the city of Atlanta. It was located in the foothills of the Blue Ridge Mountains and the Chattahoochee River ran through the rolling hills a few miles from the city. The people seemed undaunted by the hardships of the war, carrying on their daily activities as best they could.

Daniel was assigned to night patrol and guard duty. He was glad he worked nights because in the afternoon he could search for Papa. So far, he had found no one who knew his father.

The days slipped away as Daniel worked and searched. It was almost Christmas and his heart grew heavy as Christmas approached. Alone for Christmas, so far from Catherine and Joey.

A new soldier was assigned to the barracks. He was often alone and was older than most of the soldiers. Daniel found out he had been discharged from the Atlanta Hospital.

"Hello," Daniel said, extending his hand. "I'm Daniel Woodall from Georgia." The man grasped Daniel's hand and said, "Good to meet you, Daniel, I'm Charlie Thornton from Alabama, Tallapoosa County."

"Why were you in the hospital?"

"I was shot in the leg," Charlie replied.

Daniel observed that Charlie walked with a slight limp and when it rained the leg ached and the limp became more noticeable.

"The doctors thought I might loose this leg when it was infected, but I prayed God would heal my leg. The doctors kept soaking Lambs' ears bandages and wrapping it everyday to draw out the infection."

"Oh, I know about Lambs' ears bandages," Daniel said. "I helped to make baskets of them while I was in the Community Center Hospital in Dalton. You might have worn one of my bandages."

They laughed over the thought of Charlie's bandages being made by Daniel.

A friendship sprang up between Charlie and Daniel. The long stays in the hospital gave them much in common. They often patrolled the streets of Atlanta together.

Daniel realized how much he missed Garth and wondered if he was alive. He was thankful for his new friend.

Charlie was a stocky built man; his complexion and hair were dark and his eyes blue. He was 38 years old and his wife's name was Catherine. They had three young sons, James, John and Milton.

Christmas Eve dawned crisp and bright. Daniel and Charlie were relieved of duty at 6:00 a.m. They walked through the quiet streets, crossed the railroad tracks at the Atlantic Railroad Station and in the distance a train whistle sounded. "Let's watch the train passengers get off," Charlie said.

"Okay," Daniel answered.

Mostly uniformed soldiers came from the train. As the last passenger moved out of the train, Daniel's heart leaped within his chest. The last man was Papa.

Running toward the train, Daniel called, "Papa, Papa. I'm here."

Tears streamed down their faces as they embraced.

""Oh, Daniel, I'm so glad to see you. I searched every list after Chickamauga and you and Garth were not listed among the dead."

"I was in a makeshift Community Center Hospital in Dalton, Papa. There were so many wounded they turned the town hall into a hospital. I wasn't shot, Papa, they found me passed out with a high fever from malaria. I left there December 1st and have been stationed here since."

"General Hood sent me to Richmond on a very important military strategy meeting. I left in the middle of the night and no one was told where I went. I'm just returning from there now," Papa said.

"Come, Papa, and meet Charlie, my new friend."

"At ease, son," Papa said, extending his hand to grip Charlie's. "Any friend of Daniel's is a friend of mine."

"I must go, boys, I have hours of briefing with General Hood, but tomorrow we will be together for Christmas Day."

"Good-bye, Papa, see you tomorrow," Daniel called as his father hurried away.

William Woodall approached the General's office with a heavy heart. He had no good news. The confederate army was in real trouble. The union army was moving to destroy the confederacy. General Sherman was a great force to be reckoned with. The confederacy was in great need of supplies and food. Many of their soldiers were barefoot and hungry.

Christmas Day 1863, Daniel and Charlie hurried to the barracks to sleep, after patrolling all night. Papa would meet them at 12:00 noon at the large Baptist Church in Atlanta. He had sent a message last night to tell them.

Daniel didn't think he would be able to sleep, but exhaustion took over and he fell into a sound sleep.

The desk sergeant tapped Daniel on the shoulder, "Better get up if you're going to be on time for the Worship Service at First Baptist."

Daniel and Charlie hurried to the old stone church and found Papa waiting on the steps.

"Good morning, boys. Hope you had a good rest."

"I didn't think I would sleep, I was so excited. But I slept like a log for five hours," Daniel replied.

As they entered the beautiful church, soft music flowed from the pipe organ. The church was almost full, many soldiers and civilians sat waiting for the worship service to begin."

Daniel stood next to his father, remembering so many wonderful Christmases as a child. The kind of Christmas he wanted to have with Joseph. Tears surfaced as Catherine and Joey entered his mind—where were they at this time? Probably they would be at Mama's house with all the family. Catherine and James would have gotten up early with Joey so he could open his gifts. Daniel could see the little log barn and all the whittled farm animals James had made.

Daniel thanked God for James as he often did. How could Catherine have managed the farm without James?

The music ended and Daniel sat listening to the soft voice of the young minister. He knew this man well, because he always attended the noon worship service on Sunday. Rev. Wente was a great comfort to the soldiers as he taught them to trust God each day.

Rev. Matthew Wente's father was a general and there had been great conflict when his young son had declared to the general that his soul had been saved by the Blood of Jesus and he did not want to be a soldier, he wanted to be a preacher. His father had always expected Matthew to follow in his footsteps. Matthew's mother had been instrumental in leading her son on the path of peace. She encouraged him to listen to God and follow his heart.

"The battle between Good and Evil will always be a part of our lives, but the Prince of Peace, Jesus, our Lord came to show us God's way. The meaning of Christmas is God's love for all mankind," the preacher said.

Papa had requested that Daniel and Charlie be allowed to eat with him in the officer's quarters. Christmas dinner was delicious. The ham was baked to perfection and the sweet potato pie melted in their mouths.

Chapter 8

Christmas, Near Death and A Wedding

Catherine and James pounded the hard shells of the black walnuts and hickory nuts. James had gathered them in the fall hiding them from the squirrels. Catherine wanted to shell them for Christmas baking. Food was getting scarce in the country. The pears were almost gone. They had been peeling two pears twice a week to have fruit with supper. Catherine had some sweet potatoes, cabbage, carrots and winter squash buried in a hole in the edge of the woods. It was hidden and covered with leaves. They had salt pork in a box under the floor in James' room. No one left meat in the smoke house any more for fear that it would be stolen in the night.

A bright ray of sunshine fell across the log where James and Catherine continued cracking nuts. Catherine's mind raced as she planned what she would take to Mama's for Christmas dinner. Tonight she would bake a Christmas nut cake. Tomorrow she would also make a baked vegetable casserole in a cream sauce. Thank God for the fresh milk daily from Bossy. Mama would bake the ham. Catherine debated if she dare use two large sweet potatoes for a pie, her better judgment won out and she decided she could not spare the potatoes. They would have the nut cake for desert.

"Now that the nuts are finished, I'm going for the Christmas tree," James said.

"I hope you can find a nice one," Catherine called after him.

"I found the perfect tree back in November. I just have a ways to go to get it home," James replied.

James hurried through the field and into the woods. He carried the ax with him and whistled in clear ringing tones. Excitement hurried him along. How lucky he was to find such a pretty holly tree with bright red berries. Catherine and Joey would love it. When he was hunting walnuts, he just happened upon the perfect Christmas tree.

A half hour walk brought James to the tree. He had brought along an old horse blanket from the barn. He quickly chopped down the small tree and wrapped the blanket around the prickly leaves. Going home would be much harder, now he had to carry the ax and balance the tree. He tied the ax to his belt giving him both hands to manage the tree.

Catherine saw James coming to the porch and ran to help.

"Oh, James, you look exhausted!" she said, as James drug the tree into the kitchen.

The blanket fell from the tree and Catherine cried, clapping her hands in excitement, "A holly tree with red berries, what a perfect tree. Joey will love it when it's decorated. As soon as he wakes from his nap, we will decorate."

The tree was set in the wooden holder and placed in the corner of the kitchen.

Catherine finished her casserole; setting it aside, she hurried to find the box that held beautiful handmade Christmas ornaments. She had received the ornaments as a wedding gift. Lifting the lid, she gazed down at the tiny angels and a sharp pain went through her heart as she remembered Daniel hanging the angels on the tree last Christmas Eve. Daniel had placed Joey's cradle near the tree so he could see each ornament as it was hung.

Closing the lid on the box, Catherine sighed. She would not cry. She wanted to be happy for James and Joey.

Darkness came early. Catherine lit the lamp and turned it low to save oil. James came from the barn, Catherine strained the milk and washed up the dishes while James took the milk to the well and lowered it down into the cold water. He filled the kitchen buckets and returned to the cozy kitchen where Catherine's nut cake was baking.

The tree was so pretty, all decorated with garland and angels. Joey and Catherine had such fun; they spent most of the afternoon decorating it.

Joey splashed water from his bathtub and squealed at James as Catherine yelled at him to stop making a mess. James grabbed a towel and mopped up the water. At last Joey was tucked into his crib.

"Time to play Santa Claus," Catherine called to James.

James came from his room carrying a large flour sack. "I'm ready," he said.

First came the little log barn, then a picket fence was placed around the barn. Next came a cow and her calf, a mama pig and three little pigs, a mare and her colt, two ducks, three geese and a dog—all stained a golden brown with walnut hulls.

Catherine stared in awe at the beautifully carved set, she had no idea James had created such a masterpiece.

She whispered softly, "James, it's beautiful! We will treasure it always."

"I think he will like it," James said.

Catherine placed her wrapped presents under the tree and James placed one wrapped gift beside the farm scene. Tomorrow was Christmas, December 25, 1863, a sad time because of the separation of war; but the message of Christmas always brought hope and joy.

A sparkling white frost covered the windowpanes in Catherine's bedroom. Jumping from bed, Catherine hurried to add wood to the stove, standing close to absorb the warmth.

Catherine heated milk and poured it into steaming mugs, she added honey and passed one to James.

"Thanks and Merry Christmas," James said.

They sat together in comfortable silence sipping the hot honey flavored milk,

"God really blessed us when you found the honey tree."

"Yes, they are rare," James answered. "I'll milk early this morning, so I can be back before Joey gets up."

"Yes, you must be here to see his face when he sees what Santa brought him," Catherine said, "I won't take him from his crib until you finish the chores."

Catherine stirred corn meal into a pan of bubbling milk stirring it slowly as it thickened into mush. She added butter, milk and honey and covered the pan.

Breakfast was ready when James returned. Joey was dressed and placed in his chair, he repeated, "Pretty tree," as he pointed at the Christmas tree. Catherine had spread a cover over the gifts until after breakfast.

James thanked God for their food.

Lifting Joey from his chair, James said, "Come on, big boy, let's see what Santa brought you for Christmas."

Catherine lifted the cover from the gifts and Joey squealed with delight as he carefully inspected each tiny figure.

"Look, Joey, open this package." Pulling open the package, Joey pulled out a little red coat.

"Mommy made it for you, try it on. Don't you look handsome in your new coat!" Catherine said.

James handed Catherine the package he had placed under the tree. She opened it slowly. Inside was an exquisite walnut chest with her name carved across the top.

"I will keep it always, James, it's beautiful!" Catherine exclaimed.

Catherine handed James his gift. "I wish it were bigger and better, because you have done so much for Joey and me," Catherine whispered.

"You know I would do anything for you and Joey, you don't need to give me anything," James replied.

James opened his gift and pulled out the handsome shirt with matching handkerchief, "You knew what I needed," James said softly.

"Go try it on, see if it fits," Catherine answered.

Turning to the table, Catherine began to clear the breakfast dishes. Her thoughts turned to Daniel, she wondered where he would spend this day. She prayed it would be a good day, and that God would bless him and keep him safe.

James returned to the kitchen, all dressed in his new clothes. "I love this shirt, it fits perfect," he said.

"You look handsome in that blue," Catherine said, smiling.

James brought the horses and wagon to the porch and loaded everything in the wagon for Mama's house. Joey chattered, "See Grandma, see Rachel and Charlie," as they rode to Mama's.

Rachel met them at the door, smiling her welcome.

"Come in, we were waiting for you to open gifts," she said.

Catherine looked at Rachel closely, she looked so pale. "Are you okay, Rachel?" she asked.

"Yes, I'm fine dear. I had some kind of spell last night and felt very weak, but I'm okay today," Rachel said.

"Rachel, up," Joey said.

Catherine watched as Rachel pulled a chair up next to the Christmas tree and sat down before she lifted Joey to her lap. A small, nagging worry circled around in Catherine's head, "Rachel looks sick."

Mama came from the kitchen and hugged Catherine and James, she dropped a kiss on the top of Joey's head.

Charlie arrived, carrying a small oak rocking chair. "Guess who this is for, Joey!" he said.

Joey slid from Rachel's lap and sat in the tiny chair. "It was given to your Papa, Joey, for his very first Christmas. Now it belongs to you. Of course, all the other children did their share of rocking in it also," Mama said.

The gifts were opened with laughter and love. Charlie and Joey went outside to play with the twine ball Rachel made for Joey. James sat engrossed in the book Mama had given him.

The Christmas goose looked and smelled superb.

"I didn't know you would roast a goose for Christmas, Mama. I thought you were baking a ham," Catherine said.

"The goose will make a fine meal, dear, I thought we would divide the ham and make many meals for your house and ours," Mama replied.

"Oh, thank you, we have so little meat left. James is making a rabbit trap. We hope he can catch some rabbits; if he does, we will share. We can't eat the chickens, because we really need the few eggs they lay. I try to give Joey and James at least two eggs a week."

Everyone gathered around the table. Mama read the Christmas story about the night God's Son came to earth from heaven to be our Savior. James asked God to watch over Papa and Daniel and thanked Him for their food and for sending us Jesus.

James loaded their gifts and food into the wagon. Catherine bundled Joey into his new coat; with arms outstretched to Rachel, he planted a wet kiss on her white cheek. Again, the worrisome little thought circled around inside Catherine's head, "Rachel does look sick."

The wagon rattled over the gravel road as they rode home in silence, Joey slept soundly on Catherine's lap.

The sun rose over the frosty meadow and the crows were already making a racket when Catherine awoke with a start. What did she hear? Not the crows, she was used to their chatter. A horse, running fast, someone was coming. Jumping from her bed, she raced to the door as Charlie bound on to the porch.

"Catherine, Mama wants you now. Rachel is very sick. Take the horse and go as fast as you can. James and I will take Joey and go to Warm Springs for Dr. Hayes."

Catherine flew to the bedroom, threw on her clothes and left immediately.

Pushing the horse as fast as she dared, Catherine raced to her dear sister. "Oh, God, hold on to Rachel," she prayed.

Tying the reins to the porch, Catherine burst through the door calling "Mama! Rachel!" There was no answer. Mama was bent over Rachel, who lay blue and quiet on the bed. "Breathe into her lungs, Catherine, I can't anymore," Mama sighed as she lay exhausted by Rachel.

Catherine pressed her mouth upon Rachel's and breathed life into Rachel's body. Her eyes flickered open, she coughed and began to breath again.

"Rachel, Rachel," Catherine cried as she held her, gently rocking her in her arms.

Dr. Hayes arrived. He had galloped at breakneck speed from Warm Springs when James had arrived at his office. He quickly examined Rachel, who seemed to be sleeping now.

"It's her heart. She had a very bad spell this time. She must have weeks of bed rest and quiet for her heart to repair."

Catherine gently led Mama to the kitchen table. She fixed the fire in the stove and made Mama some confederate coffee, strong and hot.

"Drink this, Mama, it will help," Catherine said.

Mama began to cry, "I was so scared, I thought she was going to die and I couldn't keep breathing for her."

"Don't cry, Mama, it has passed now and Dr. Hayes will tell us what to do to make Rachel better."

Rachel lay still and white upon her bed day after day. Mama and Catherine spooned hot broth and soft foods into her mouth encouraging her to eat a little more.

Jacob White came early one morning asking if he could sit with Rachel. He had known Rachel all his life; as children, they had attended the one-room school in Warm Springs together. He often sat on the school steps with Rachel at recess because she couldn't run and play in the hot sun. He had always loved the little girl who seemed to have so much love inside of her.

When Rachel was seventeen, he had asked her to marry him. Her beautiful blue eyes filled with tears and she turned him down because she said he needed a strong, healthy wife who could help him farm.

Soon after, Jake was called away to war. War was hell and he had thought often of Rachel. The night his arm was destroyed he had thought he would die, but he didn't die. After months in the Atlanta Hospital, he had been discharged and sent home. He never went to see Rachel because now he knew he couldn't take care of her.

Catherine brushed Rachel's hair and tied it with the blue ribbon she had bought her long ago. A bit of color had returned to Rachel's face.

"Jacob's coming to spend the afternoon with you and read to you. Aren't you two ever going to finish that book?" Catherine giggled.

Rachel smiled a sweet smile. "Oh, we read some times," she said, "and sometimes we just talk. He has asked me to marry him, Catherine, he says we need each other. With my bad heart and his one arm, do you think we could make a life together?"

Catherine grabbed Rachel in a big hug. "Oh, of course," she replied, "you could have a great life together, love always makes a way."

"I'm so happy for you, Rachel. Jacob is a kind, wonderful man and while you finish recovering we can plan a wedding."

"Don't tell Mama yet, Jacob wants to talk to her. He's afraid Mama will think he can't take care of me."

"Rachel, Mama loves Jake. You know she will approve."

The wedding was set for March 5th. Mama cried when she realized Papa wouldn't be there to give away the bride. James said he would stand in for Papa.

Mama came to Rachel's room carrying a large box.

"If we only have six weeks to plan a wedding, we had better get busy." Lifting the lid from the box and folding back the white sheet, they looked down on Mama's wedding gown.

"Oh, Mama, I had forgotten how beautiful your gown was, do you think it will fit me?" Rachel asked.

"I'm sure we will have to take in the waist, you have lost a lot of weight since this sickness. The length should be good, since we are almost the same height," Mama answered.

"When Catherine comes, we will have a fitting session and decide what Catherine will wear as your attendant. James can wear Papa's good suit, I will need to hem the pants."

"We must have dear old Reverend Roper for the ceremony. You know he married Papa and me, but he may not be well enough to come. If not, we will ask his son. He is also a minister. We had such a good time when Rev. Roper came and married Daniel and Catherine. All his family came." Mama said.

A soft blush had spread across Rachel's cheeks while Mama planned. Hope was born anew. She and Jake would have a good life together; she would leave her bad heart in God's hands and live her life to the fullest.

"The Warm Springs Primitive Baptist Church will be beautiful on March 5th, Mama. Jake and I will gather that shiny green vine that grows along the creek banks. The narcissus will be in bloom. We will gather them from the field behind Jake's mom's house. The entire altar will be wrapped in green with French knots of narcissus intertwined. Won't it be wonderful?" Rachel exclaimed.

"You can't overdo, dear, maybe Charlie had better gather the vine, but I'm sure you and Jake could pick the flowers," Mama said.

A warm breeze drifted across the Georgia countryside in mid-February, bringing a touch of green.

James came from the barn with the horses and wagon. Since it was a nice day, Catherine had decided they would go to Mama's and finish planning Rachel's wedding.

Rachel met them at the door. Catherine marveled at the change in her. Her eyes sparkled and there was a soft glow on her cheeks.

Rachel danced around the kitchen with Joey.

"My, how you are growing, every time I see you, you're bigger!"

Joey laughed with delight, to have Rachel well again.

James and Charlie left to mend fences, leaving the girls to have their fitting session.

Lifting the heavy satin material over Rachel's head, Catherine pulled the gown into place.

"Rachel, you look absolutely wonderful, the gown fits perfect. Mama did a great job altering it," Catherine cried. "Stand in front of the mirror and I will call Mama."

Mama stood in the doorway crying, overcome with joy and sadness. How she wished Papa could be here for Rachel's wedding.

Hugging Rachel, Mama said, "How quickly you grew from childhood to a beautiful bride. Now, come see Joey, he's waiting in my room."

Joey stood in the middle of Mama's bed dressed in a little black suit with tails and a bow tie. He was very pleased with his new clothes.

"Mama, where did you ever get such a perfect outfit for Joey!" Catherine exclaimed.

"I made it from one of Papa's black coats. It took some doing to get all the pieces cut. I made the pattern with all his measurements and just started cutting. I also altered this blue gown for you, Catherine, and now I think we are ready for a wedding."

Chapter 9

Going Home

Daniel approached the barracks on a mild February evening. He missed Charlie who had been sent on a patrol last week. He wished he could have gone with Charlie, but only a few soldiers were picked for the patrol.

The desk sergeant was busy with paper work. As Daniel passed, he glanced up and said, "Daniel, a note from your father came today."

Daniel accepted the note, wondering what was happening with Papa. He had not seen him for weeks.

> *Daniel,*
>
> *General Hood has discovered there is someone in Oglethorpe who is an informer to the union army. He has chosen me to go because I am familiar with the country. I am to try and find the source by giving out some untrue information, which they will be waiting to receive. I have requested that you come with me and he has agreed. We will be able to go home on the weekend. Meet me at the Atlantic Railway Station at 7:00 p.m. tonight.*
>
> *Papa*

The desk sergeant smiled and said, "I know, Daniel, I have already processed your papers. You better hurry and get your things together. You have two hours to be at the station."

The few belongings were quickly packed into a duffle bag. "I must be dreaming," Daniel thought, because he could not yet believe that he would be leaving Atlanta to go to Oglethorpe, which was only twenty miles from Catherine.

It was dark when Daniel reached the station. Papa waved from the platform. "Come on, I have our tickets. We leave in 40 minutes," he called.

The passenger car was almost empty when they entered; a few other passengers came aboard. The train whistle sounded and the train moved slowly from the station. Daniel thought, "I'm not dreaming, I really am going home."

The train gathered speed, roaring through the dark countryside. A bright moon rose over the treetops. Papa slept, but sleep would not come to Daniel. His longing to be with Catherine became a physical pain, sleep was impossible.

Dawn streaked the eastern sky as the train pulled into Macon Station. Papa roused Daniel, who had finally fallen asleep.

"We will get off the train here and have breakfast. The train from Oglethorpe won't arrive until noon," Papa said.

Breakfast tasted so good to Daniel, biscuits, brown gravy and scrambled eggs. He had eaten army food for so long, he had almost forgotten how good home cooking was. The shopkeeper felt bad there was no coffee, only milk.

The train from Oglethorpe was on time. It would leave at noon to return to Oglethorpe.

The conductor asked the passengers to pray that their trip would be safe. They would pass through country besieged by the union army and they often blew up the railroad tracks. Daniel and Papa prayed together.

There were milling soldiers in the Oglethorpe Station. Daniel wondered why there was so much activity in the middle of the night, and then he realized they were young soldiers, only boys seventeen and eighteen years old from Training Camp on their way to war. They laughed and joked. Daniel thought about when he left Eufala a year ago, the horror of Chickamauga surfacing in his mind.

The Davon Hotel was tastefully luxurious. Daniel took in the rich grandeur as Papa arranged for their room. Whoever owned this hotel had money, which was pretty scarce in this time of war.

A bell rang overhead and a fastidious black man came down the stairs. "Good evening, I am Isaac. I will show you to your room," he said.

As soon as the door was closed, Daniel whispered, "Is he a slave?"

"I'm sure he is," Papa replied.

"He seemed so dignified, I always thought of slaves as field hands."

"Wealthy people have well trained slaves to run their homes and work in their businesses."

"I don't believe anyone should be a slave," Daniel said.

"Neither do I, son, but I doubt anyone will ask our opinion on the subject. Power, money and politics are what this war is all about. The plantation owners need slaves to gain more power, produce more cotton and make more money and so it goes in the world we live in."

"In the hotel, I will be known as Jonathan Wren and you are my son, John. We are government agents working for General Lee on orders to locate a place for some strategic military plans to take place. General Hood's undercover men set it all up. They are waiting for the leak to come back to them and then they will close in on the informant."

Mr. Davon, owner of the hotel, met Daniel and Papa in the dining room.

"Good morning, my clerk tells me you are working for General Lee," he said. His charming smile invited Papa to tell him all about being a government agent.

Daniel observed Mr. Davon silently, his black hair lay in perfect waves and he was immaculate, but for some unknown reason Daniel felt a cold distaste for this man. He was relieved when Mr. Davon left their table.

"Tomorrow, we leave to find that military place," Papa said. "We will need to rent a buggy for three days and what we are really doing is going home."

The buggy was comfortable and Daniel was happy to have this time to talk to Papa. "How long do you think this war will last?" he asked.

"The confederacy has so few resources, England has refused to take up our cause. They need our cotton, but they don't think slavery is right; so to get involved in our war makes the price for cotton too high," Papa answered.

"I wish General Lee would surrender so we could come home for good."

"Lee is a fine man and a brilliant military planner, but his soldiers are hungry and their uniforms and shoes are wearing out and no one knows where the money will come from to replace them," Papa said.

"So many have died. I don't want to fight anymore. I agree with England. People should not have to be slaves." Daniel replied.

"We are committed, Daniel, until it is settled one way or the other. Most likely, the union will win this war and slavery will be abolished and that is good, but so many more men will die before it's all over." Papa stated sadly.

Evening shadows lengthened as they turned into the road that led to Daniel and Catherine's home.

A warm March wind had swept over Georgia and the spring blossoms had appeared.

Catherine sat in the twilight waiting for James and Joey to return from their walk to the creek. Joey wanted to see the tadpoles that would turn to frogs.

A cool breeze caressed Catherine's face as she sat resting. Someone was coming up the lane. Fear griped her; it could be union soldiers, though not likely in a buggy. She calmed herself and strained her eyes to see better. The men getting out of the buggy seemed so familiar. It couldn't be, Daniel and Papa.

Jumping to her feet, Catherine raced to the buggy. Daniel ran to meet her and clasped her in his arms, his lips closing over hers. "Catherine, my beloved, I have missed you so," he whispered.

Catherine walked between Papa and Daniel holding each of their arms. She could not yet believe they were really here.

James and Joey came around the porch. James let out a whoop of joy as he gathered his father in a bear hug, then Daniel.

Daniel knelt down in front of Joey and Catherine joined him. "Joey, this is your Papa," Catherine said.

Joey reached out his chubby hands and touched Daniel's face. "Papa cry," he said.

Daniel opened his arms and said, "Only because I am so happy to see you and Mama again."

Catherine lifted Joey into Daniel's arms and they all went into the house together.

"The wedding, Catherine, they are here for the wedding," James cried.

"Oh, my goodness, I forgot all about the wedding. Rachel is being married on Saturday. Mama will be so happy that you can walk her down the aisle, she cried because you would miss the wedding. Can you believe that you are here for the wedding!" Catherine exclaimed.

"Rachel is getting married? To whom?" Papa asked.

"Jacob White. He was wounded, lost the lower part of his left arm in combat and was sent home," James answered.

"Jake always loved Rachel. I'm glad she's marrying him. He will be a good husband. It's a good thing I have my uniform since I am to be in a wedding," Papa said.

"Come on, James, let's you and I go and surprise Mama, Rachel and Charlie."

Joey took Daniel's hand and led him to the corner of the kitchen to see all of his toys. They sat together on the floor and examined each of the hand carved animals in the farm set.

Catherine bathed Joey and put on his nightshirt, they sat together and read from the Bible. When Daniel's picture fell from the Bible, Joey said "Papa come home."

Daniel tucked Joey into his crib and turned to Catherine. "Oh, my beloved, I have dreamed of this moment so many times," he said as he gathered her into his arms. The door of the bedroom clicked shut.

The rooster crowed, the crows squabbled and golden rays of sunlight fell across the bed. Catherine opened her eyes and joy flooded her soul as she looked at Daniel's face cradled on the pillow next to her. Daniel was home only for a short time, but these days were a gift from God. They would spend every moment together as a family.

Daniel stirred and opened his eyes. He gathered Catherine into his arms and said, "It's hard to believe I am really here."

Joey appeared beside the bed. "I'm hungry," he said.

"Hungry, little man. No wonder you are growing so big," Daniel said as he lifted him into the bed. Joey squealed with delight and the tussle was on.

Catherine prepared breakfast, Daniel brought the Bible to the table and he and Joey looked at the picture again. The picture brought sad memories of Garth to Daniel.

"I never heard from Garth after Chickamauga. He was a good friend and I loved him like he was my brother. I never knew anyone who could draw like he could," Daniel said, staring at his own reflection.

"Perhaps you will meet again someday," Catherine said softly.

James and Charlie arrived in the buggy. Daniel greeted his little brother, exclaiming over how much he had grown.

"Mama wants everyone to come home for supper tonight, she is ever so anxious to see Daniel and we can all go over the wedding plans with Rachel and Jake. Rachel's just floating on air, she's so happy Papa is home for her wedding," James said.

Daniel swung Joey to his shoulder, "Come on, boys, let's go check out that new calf you named after me," he said.

"She's a nice heifer," James answered. "It was Catherine's idea to name her Dannybelle."

Catherine cleaned the kitchen and went to her bedroom. She knelt down beside her bed and thank God for allowing Daniel and Papa to come home for this brief time.

James, Charlie and Joey took the wagon, leaving the buggy for Catherine and Daniel.

The birds sang, and Catherine's heart sailed with the soft clouds in the blue sky as she and Daniel rode slowly along on this perfect spring day.

Mama and Papa worked together in the kitchen, supper was almost ready when the family arrived.

The smell of roasted chicken and sweet potatoes made Catherine hungry. Charlie went to the well to bring the cold milk.

Papa and Daniel went to greet Jacob as he arrived.

The supper was blessed and eaten with joyful thanksgiving that God had given them this time together.

"Tomorrow begins early," Mama said. "Charlie and James will gather the vine for the church altar. Rachel and Jake will take tubs and gather the narcissus. Catherine, you and Daniel and Joey take the buggy and go look for the early blooming honeysuckle over near Pine Bluff. Papa and I have a neighbor roasting the pig, so we will be free to make the potato salad. Mrs. Hayes has made the wedding cake. Everyone will be at the church by noon to decorate. Then home by two to dress and back to the church for the ceremony at 4:30."

Rachel hugged Mama and said, "I'm so excited I'm about to burst!"

The altar was a work of art. Rachel had twined the vines around each spindle and the clusters of narcissus smelled divine.

"Daniel, bring the vases for the honeysuckle," Catherine called as she placed the tub by the church door.

"Oh, Catherine, isn't the church beautiful and doesn't it smell like you think heaven will smell? Can you believe I'm really going to marry Jake and Papa is here to give me to Jake and Daniel is here to be your escort? James will be Jake's best man and Joey will carry my wedding ring to the altar!"

"Slow down, Rachel, you are way too excited," Catherine laughed.

Mama cried as Rachel floated down the aisle on Papa's arm.

Chapter 10

Time Stood Still

Three days of bliss had passed for Catherine and Daniel, being with Mama and Papa, seeing Rachel married and the joyful wedding supper.

Everyone had stayed all night at Mama's on Saturday so they would be there to see Rachel and Jacob off on Sunday morning. They would be staying a week with Jake's family. Then they would live with Mama until Papa returned from the war.

The wagon bounced as Daniel turned the horses into the lane.

Daniel and Catherine sat on the wagon seat. James, Charlie and Joey lay on a quilt in the back of the wagon. Catherine was quiet, letting the laughing and teasing flow around her. This is the way life is supposed to be, she thought. The warm afternoon sun made Catherine's skin tingle with the pure joy of being here with her family.

Daniel and Papa would return to Oglethorpe early tomorrow, but they would come home again on Thursday.

"James, if you bring one of Papa's plows home this week, we can both plow when I get back. If we don't get a rainy spell, we should be able to get our cotton planted before I return to Atlanta," Daniel said.

The fields were plowed and the cotton planted.

James said at supper, "Hey, Catherine, I think I'll trade you in for Daniel for a helper in the cotton field. I didn't have to wait for him a single time while he daydreamed about spinning."

Daniel asked, "What's this about spinning and daydreaming?"

James supplied all the fun details of Catherine's daydreaming.

Moving to Catherine's side, Daniel wrapped his arm around her waist and said, "I really don't know how you two have managed this farm so well."

"If it hadn't been for James, I would have had to move in with Mama and the farm would be overgrown with weed," Catherine said.

"I think there is as much bravery on the home front as there is on the battlefield," Daniel answered.

"Joey, all those tadpoles have shed their tails, do you want to go see the frogs they turned into?" James asked.

Joey squealed, "See frogs!" He scrambled from his chair and ran to James. "Bye, Mama. Bye, Papa," he said as he grasped James' hand and started for the door.

"Let's clean this kitchen and go for a walk to the beech trees," Daniel said.

Hand in hand they crossed the field and strolled up the knoll to the grove of beech trees.

Catherine traced the heart with their names carved inside with her finger.

"Can you believe it's only been a year since you left, Daniel."

"It seems like a lifetime ago," she continued.

They sat on a mossy log and talked.

"How long before the war will be over?"

"Papa thinks at least another year, but, of course, no one knows for sure. He also thinks the confederate will lose; we don't have the resources, manpower or money to beat the union. I believe slavery is wrong, Catherine," Daniel said.

"I agree, Daniel, but how awful for the confederate soldiers to fight a war they can't win," Catherine cried.

"Yes, don't you wish they would just surrender now, think how many will die in another year. War is so awful and so lonely. I made a new friend in Atlanta. His name is Charlie Thornton. He almost lost his leg and was in the Atlanta Hospital for a long time. When he was released, he came to our company. We work together at night. His wife's name is Catherine. He was sent on a mission just before I left Atlanta. I was disappointed that I wasn't picked to go with them, but if I had gone I would not have been there to come home with Papa."

"God has a plan and we are following that plan, that's why you were not chosen to go with Charlie," Catherine answered.

Daniel smiled down on Catherine and stroked her hair gently.

"Tomorrow, we will go to see Mama and Papa, James and I will help to plant their cotton," Daniel said.

Mama and Papa sat on the porch. Catherine handed Mama a big bouquet of wild Sweet Williams they had stopped and picked for her.

"I'm glad you're here, Daniel, you and I can go buy four pigs, a farmer not too far away has a liter ready to wean. We will get two for Mama and two for Catherine," Papa said.

"Oh, Papa, thank you, I wanted to buy a pair of pigs but the cotton money is almost gone and I just couldn't afford them. Now we will have meat for winter," Catherine said.

"You're welcome, I'm glad Mama and I can help you and Daniel," Papa answered.

Papa and Charlie, Daniel and James worked together planting Mama's cotton fields. The days were warm and sunny and except for the scarcity of many foods, it seemed the war had never come.

Catherine knew the days were running out and Papa and Daniel would be going back to Atlanta after one more weekend.

Daniel wanted to do something special for Catherine before he left. A surprise was planned between him and James. They were gathering stones from the creek every chance they had. On Thursday evening they took the wagon to the creek and loaded all the stones.

Catherine asked, "What are you going to do with all those stones?"

Daniel stopped the horses in the middle of the front yard.

"We are going to build the flowerbed I promised you long ago. When we were waiting to go into battle at Chickamauga, I remembered I never took time to build your flower bed. Today you shall have your desire," Daniel said.

"Oh, Daniel, in such a time you thought about a flowerbed," Catherine cried.

"Yes, dear, I wished so much I had built if for you because I didn't know if I would ever come home," Daniel answered.

The stones were chipped and faced and Daniel built a beautiful round bed. James returned from the woods with the wagon filled with rich black soil.

While Catherine cooked supper, Daniel hurried to the barn and brought a red rose bush Mama had dug from her yard. Then he called Catherine to come and see.

Crying with joy, Catherine walked around the bed. She asked, "Daniel, where did you get a rose bush?"

"Mama wanted you to have it, she dug it from her back yard," Daniel said.

"I simply cannot believe it—a flower bed and a rose bush all in one day!" Catherine exclaimed. Throwing her arms around Daniel in a great hug, she sang, "Thank you for such a wonderful gift."

Joey danced with them, laughing and clapping his hands. He wasn't so sure why they were all so happy, but he loved the excitement.

James sat on the wagon seat watching them. He thought how sad Catherine and Mama would be when Papa and Daniel returned to war. He prayed, "God, go with them and bring them back to us."

Saturday morning, James decided he would go and spend the day with Mama and Papa. Joey was invited to come along and play with Charlie.

"You be a good boy," Daniel said as he lifted Joey to the wagon seat.

"Bye, Papa," Joey called as the wagon rattled away.

Daniel stood alone on the porch, this would be his last time alone with Catherine for a long time. He had so many feelings inside. He didn't want to go back to war, but he knew he must. Papa was an officer and an officer's son would never go AWOL.

Catherine was finishing the dishes when Daniel entered the kitchen. Picking up the water bucket, she asked, "Want to come with me to the well?"

Daniel took the bucket and followed her to the well; he set the bucket down and clasped Catherine' hand.

"Let's walk before we get the water," he said.

As they rounded the house, Catherine observed that one of the buds on the rose bush had opened into a beautiful rose.

"Daniel, look at the rose, it's like a sign from God. It will be there blooming when you return."

Slowly they walked through the cotton field checking the tiny plants, poking their heads through the red clay soil.

"It won't be long until time to start chopping the cotton," Catherine said.

"How will you and James ever do all the work, how can you watch Joey and work in the fields?"

"Rachel will help me with Joey, she loves him dearly, somehow we will manage."

They crossed the creek on stepping-stones and wandered down a path through deep woods, at last they stopped and sat on a fallen log to rest. Daniel gathered Catherine in his arms and moaned, "I don't want to leave you tomorrow. I will miss you and Joey so desperately."

Catherine caressed his face and kissed his lips—for the moment time stood still and they were one, and the war was forgotten.

Daniel brought the water bucket to the kitchen; Catherine started the fresh peas they had shelled. She would take them to Mama's for supper. It would be their last meal together for a long time. She chopped the wild onions and added them to the boiling peas.

James and Joey arrived to pick up Daniel and Catherine. The food was packed. They were hungry and ready to eat. When they smelled supper, they were glad they were hungry. Mama had fried platters of breaded catfish.

"Where in the world did you ever get fresh catfish?" Catherine cried.

"Papa bought it in Warm Springs today. Isn't it wonderful to have something different for a change," Mama exclaimed.

Rachel and Jacob arrived and the men carried the table and chairs outside under the big maple tree. Papa blessed the food as they stood holding hands.

"Mama, you have outdone yourself, never have I tasted better fish," Daniel said.

The mood at dinner was joyful, everyone talked and laughed, but in every heart and mind was the thought that tomorrow they would go back to war.

Papa's leak in Oglethorpe had come back to the undercover men in General Hood's company. Papa and Daniel had received a telegraph telling them to return to Atlanta.

Mama and Daniel strolled to the vegetable garden; Catherine could see they were having a serious conversation. She was so glad Daniel was close to his mother; she hoped she and Joey would always be close as Mama was to all her children.

The food was put away, the table and chairs returned to the kitchen. The evening sun died in a blaze of orange and purple as they prepared to go home.

Joey was tired and cranky when they arrived home. He fussed while Catherine bathed him; finished at last, she lifted him into Daniel's arms.

Daniel pulled the rocking chair into the circle of light from the lamp. He lifted the Bible from the stand and opened it to the picture of himself.

"Papa must go tomorrow, Joey, I don't want to go but I must for I am a soldier and I have to go back to my job. I will miss you and Mama very much. I will come home when my job is finished. I want you and Mama to look at my picture every day and pray for me."

"Luv you, Papa," Joey said. Daniel rocked him until he was sound asleep. He tucked him into his crib and returned to Catherine.

"Come outside and walk with me in the moonlight," Daniel requested.

Already a relentless, mind-numbing pain burned in Catherine's chest, Daniel must go and she could not make it harder for him.

The moonlight was soft and shimmering, casting shadows across Catherine's face as Daniel's eyes drew her to him.

They stood by the flowerbed locked in an embrace, rocking back and forth, the pain of parting was almost unbearable.

Dawn tinged the eastern sky when Catherine heard Papa's buggy coming. Daniel was ready. They would not wake Joey.

Daniel lifted his duffle bag, kissed Catherine sweetly and said softly, "See you soon, my love."

Catherine smiled up at him and said, "I'll be waiting right here."

She walked with him to the buggy, hugged and kissed Papa and the buggy pulled away.

Catherine stood on the porch until the last sound of the buggy died away in the distance, then she collapsed to the steps, sobbing, "Oh, God, bring him back to me. Lift me up and carry me forward until that time."

Papa turned to Daniel and said, "Catherine will be okay, Mama and the family will help her."

Daniel nodded his head, afraid to speak for fear the burning sob in his throat would burst forth.

Chapter 11

War and Destruction

As the train roared through the night, Daniel relived his time at home. He stored each memory away. They would have to last him for a long time. In times of great distress, he would draw strength from these memories.

April 17, 1864, the train pulled into the Atlantic Railway Terminal of Atlanta. The weather was hot for springtime.

An officer Papa knew stopped to talk as they got off the train.

"Did you hear the latest news, Billie?" he asked.

"No, I have been to Oglethorpe, what is the news?" Papa asked.

"Today, General Hood received a telegram telling him General Grant stopped all prisoner exchanges. This will surely increase our manpower shortages. I suppose all captured confederates will be sent to that awful union prison in Rock Island, Illinois," the officer said.

Daniel shuddered as he listed to the sad news.

Papa hugged Daniel and hurried away to report to General Hood. Daniel moved toward the barracks in a fog. His brain registered little, he simply moved forward. He reported to the desk sergeant that his mission with Papa had been completed.

"Glad you had a safe journey. Things have really heated up since you left. Looks like we will see a lot of action soon," the sergeant said.

"You won't be walking patrol anymore, all soldiers have been ordered to build Gabions to fortify Atlanta against Sherman," he said.

"What are Gabions?" Daniel asked.

They are huge woven open-ended basket filled with dirt. Hopefully, they will stop a bullet or slow down a cannonball. The army is trying to put emplacements on all the approaches to Atlanta. Right now, they are working on Tallulah Street, you will report there tomorrow morning," the sergeant continued.

The sun was hot and sweat streaked Daniel's dirty face as he shoveled dirt into Gabions. Yes, he thought he would be glad to have these things between him and Sherman's army.

Tired and dirty, Daniel and the other soldiers returned to the barracks.

The desk sergeant called to him as he entered the hallway. "Hey, remember the patrol that left; just before you left with your Papa? The one your friend, Charlie, went on. We got a wire today that they were all captured at Big Shanty, Georgia. They were in a military prison in Louisville, Kentucky for a few days, but General Grant will no longer do prisoner exchanges, so they have been sent to Rock Island, Illinois," the sergeant said.

Tears filled Daniel's eyes as he turned away, remembering all the nights he and Charlie had talked about going home to their Catherines. He would pray everyday for Charlie and Garth.

Sherman's army was on the move. 100,000 union soldiers left Chattanooga, Tennessee on May 5th. Three Generals led the armies, Schofield, McPherson and the Rock of Chickamauga, George Thomas.

Moving against the union army was General Joe Johnston's army of Tennessee with 60,000 men led by Hardee, Polk and Hood.

Sherman's army pushed southward following the Western and Atlantic Railway.

Daniel's regiment, under General Hood, fought valiantly; often they were so hungry the only thought they had was how to stop the ache in their gut.

General Polk, who had been an Episcopal Bishop, stopped fighting long enough to baptize General Johnston and General Hood. On Pine Mountain on June 14, 1864, he went home to Jesus; he was killed by a federal cannonball. It was a sad day for the confederates, the soldiers grieved for the fallen priest.

Sherman's army was met at Peach Tree Creek by General Hood's army on July 20th. The fighting was furious and bloody. Over 4,000 confederates died. Sherman's army also had heavy losses, but still they pushed on, arriving in Atlanta on July 22nd. Daniel's troops lay in the trenches they had built around Atlanta.

The thought of dying seemed a comfort to Daniel, no more pain, no more watching others died, no more hunger. The desire to stand up and let a bullet rip through him seemed like maybe the easy way out. Then the memory of he and Catherine and Joey dancing around the flowerbed drifted through his mind. No, he would not die, he would fight and somehow God would help him to survive this awful war and he would go home.

Ten long, terrible days they fought trying to hold Atlanta, so many had died. Still, Sherman's army pounded them.

On September 1st, General Hood gave the order to evacuate Atlanta. There was mass hysteria as the people fled trying to carry what little belongings they could get out.

On September 2nd, Sherman took command of Atlanta. This was a tremendous boost to the union and devastating to General Hood's army.

The morale of Daniel's regiment was at an all-time low. The question "Where do we go from here?" seemed to hang in the air.

General Hood led his men on an attack of the Federal supply lines north of Atlanta, they came to Dalton, Georgia. As Daniel fought his way through Dalton, he stopped in front of the Community Center that had once been a hospital. He thought of Sarah and prayed she was some place safe away from the fighting.

General Hood made the decision to move his men to Tennessee in the hope of drawing Sherman out of Georgia, but Sherman turned back to Atlanta and on November 16, 1884, he left the burning city and started his terrible march of destruction across Georgia, 60 miles wide and 300 miles long with little opposition. Many slaves followed Sherman's army dancing and singing, for their day of freedom had finally arrived.

November 30th dawned cold and clear as Daniel's unit fought General Schofield's army. They fought desperately. Daniel knew they were in a great crisis as the battle raged around him. He repeated the long ago command "Forward with Courage" to himself over and over.

Five great confederate generals died that day. The story told on the battlefield was, they had breakfast together in the morning and that night they were corpses on the back porch of McGaveck Mansion. Five thousand, five hundred confederate soldiers were killed or wounded that day.

Daylight filtered through the leaves over his face, Daniel lifted his head and listened. The only sound he heard was the gentle rustle of the leaves in a slight breeze and somewhere nearby he could hear the trickle of water.

Daniel sat up trying to remember how he came to be in this place. The slaughter of yesterday came flooding back. The union army just kept coming over the confederate entrenchment. There were so many they could not be stopped. The men were given orders to retreat; each soldier was on his own as they fled for their lives. Daniel remembered running, falling, stumbling until he reached the cover of the woods. Then he crawled on in the darkness until he finally dropped in exhaustion in the deep underbrush.

As the first rays of sun touched Daniel's face, he sat up. He was so thirsty, but he did not feel hungry; his stomach had been empty so long it no longer ached. The briars tore at his face but he crawled on, too weak to stand. At last he reached a clearing and there was a spring. Burying his face in the cold water, he drank, then lay resting beside the spring. He knew that if he was to live he must find food.

Chapter 12

A New Life Begins

Soft April showers watered the Georgia cotton fields causing the young cotton plants to grow and also the weeds.

Catherine rolled over in bed, the sound of the rain lulled her back into a light sleep. She blinked her eyes open and a wave of nausea swept over her.

Jumping from her bed, Catherine raced to the front porch and relieved herself of everything that was in her stomach. Clinging to the porch rail, she continued to heave.

A slow dawning came to Catherine's mind, "I am with child." A shiver of excitement passed over her, another child she and Daniel would share together, perhaps a little sister for Joey.

Catherine sank to the steps holding her head, as reality flooded over her. The cotton needed chopped, Joey was lots of work, she must cook and do laundry and keep the vegetable garden free of weeds, and pick and prepare the food from the garden.

Daniel would not be here to hold her when the time came for the baby to be born. She must bear all that pain alone. Catherine wept.

Catherine heard James remove the milk pail from its hook. He was dressed and ready to do barn chores. She must dress and prepare breakfast.

Another wave of nausea passed over Catherine as she thought of frying eggs.

James sharpened the hoes and leaned them against the porch. "Almost time to start chopping the cotton," he commented.

"Yes, the rain really made the weeds grow. I know we can't let the weeds get bigger than the cotton or we will never get it worked out," Catherine answered.

"Are you sleeping well, you have dark circles under your eyes?" James asked.

"I'm fine, just a little tired today," Catherine replied.

"I'll take the wagon and go help Mama today. Jacob is amazing with all the things he can do with one arm and a stub, but he can't chop cotton."

"I'm so glad Mama and Rachel have Jacob to help with their farm chores. Mama said he could milk the cow in no time at all," Catherine said.

"When I return from Mama's, I will leave the wagon in the tree line behind the field. We will need a place for Joey to play and nap while we work the fields. It will be cool there in the shade. If I can get everything ready, we will start chopping the cotton early in the morning," James said.

Mama and Charlie were in the field when James arrived. Taking a hoe from the barn, he greeted them and started chopping the row next to Mama.

"James it is so good to see you, how are Catherine and Joey this morning?" Mama asked.

"Catherine is sick and I'm worried about her," James answered.

Mama looked at James with concern, "How is she sick, what are her symptoms?" she asked.

"She is throwing up every morning and has dark circles under her eyes. She looks so tired," James continued.

"When did the vomiting start?" Mama asked.

"It's been going on nearly a month and I'm afraid, what would we do if Catherine died?" James replied worriedly.

Mama dropped her hoe and gathered James in her arms as tears slid down his cheeks. "Oh, James, Catherine is not going to die, she is going to have a baby. Soon the morning sickness will pass and she will be fine. In about eight months, Joey will have a little brother or sister," Mama said.

"A baby," James said.

"Yes, dear, a baby. Daniel was home in March and now Catherine is expecting a second child."

A slow smile spread over James' face. "Not death, but life," he said, a great load lifting from his young shoulders. Joey would not lose his mama, he would have a brother or sister.

"Life is good," James said.

Picking up his hoe, he chopped happily at the weeds.

"Papa said the war would probably be over in a year. We can do it, Mama, we will be here taking care of the farms when Papa and Daniel return, and there will be a new baby," James said.

Catherine listened while James made plans for the coming week. All she wanted to do was crawl between her cool sheets and close her eyes. She debated if she would tell James about the child. Not for a while, she decided.

The cotton must be cleared of weeds, so the plants could grow. Once the plants reached a certain height, they would shade out most of the weeds. It was vital the chopping start now.

The early light of a new day awakened Catherine. The nausea that always came as soon as she rolled over washed over her. She munched on the dry bread she had placed beside her bed and waited for the morning sickness to subdue.

Joey had adapted to the early morning schedule of going to the field. He was wide-awake as soon as Catherine lifted him from his bed, after breakfast he was ready to go outside.

James lifted Joey to his shoulders and said, "Come on, Big Boy, let's get a move on. You toad friend is probably looking for you."

"See Toadie Frog," Joey exclaimed.

On their first day in the field, Joey had found a large brown toad hopping among the cotton plants. James had shown Joey how to stick his bare little foot in the soft soil and pat the soil firmly over his foot. When James gently pulled his foot from the firm soil, it remained in place leaving a small dirt house.

James placed the frog in the tiny house and said, "Now the toad has a house."

Joey giggled with delight and built Toadie houses all along the row.

The sun was hot as Catherine worked her way down the row chopping out the weeds and thinning the cotton where it was too thick. She stopped to watch Joey playing in the dirt. As she watched, a large black and yellow butterfly drifted toward him. It landed on a cotton plant just inches from his face. He stuck out his hand and, wonder of wonders, the butterfly climbed on his hand. Catherine held her breath as she observed the look of utter amazement on Joey's face. Standing perfectly still, he watched the slow rhythm of the wings. Suddenly, the butterfly rose into the air and sailed away.

Joey ran after the butterfly until it was out of sight.

"Butterfly, Mama," he called to Catherine.

"Yes, Joey, I saw the butterfly. It was very special that it landed on your hand."

By ten o'clock, Joey was tired and ready for his nap. James encouraged Catherine to get into the cool shaded wagon and rest with Joey until he fell asleep.

Catherine wiped Joey's face, hands and dirty little feet. He ate his butter bread, nestled beside Catherine and was soon fast asleep. He would sleep until noon. Then they would go to the house for dinner.

Dark clouds formed in the western sky, and a brisk wind sprang up. James and Catherine watched the clouds.

"Looks like we may get rained out," James said.

Catherine jumped when a loud crack of lightening and thunder vibrated across the sky. Looking toward the wagon, she saw Joey frightened and crying.

Dropping her hoe, Catherine raced to the wagon and wrapped Joey in his bedding. James brought the hoes and they ran toward the house. Lightening continued to flash with loud peals of thunder and the wind blew furiously.

James gasped when he saw the funnel cloud swirling toward them. What could they do? The force of the wind was so strong. The mound of dirt formed by the Terrace Row in the cotton field was their only hope. The roar of the wind sounded like a train coming. The sky turned a strange green color.

Catherine stopped, she stood clutching Joey to her breast, staring in horror at the coming tornado.

Grabbing Catherine, James screamed above the roar of the wind, "Get down into the ditch."

Catherine fell into the ditch, pulling Joey's blanket over their heads.

The rain fell in sheets, but the roaring sound had ceased. The monster tornado had not touched down. The house and barn still stood, and they were not injured.

Catherine lifted her muddy face up to God and breathed a prayer of thanksgiving. They had been spared.

Joey crawled from between Catherine and James and said, "Joey scared!"

James and Catherine burst into laughter as they gathered their muddy blanket and hoes and went home.

The rain continued through the night and into the second day. The field was muddy and it would be days before they could go on with the cotton chopping.

The rainy mornings were a welcome relief to Catherine. She pulled boxes from under her bed and brought out the baby clothes she and Mama had sewn for Joey. If the new baby was a boy, she would need very little; if a girl, then she would make some dainty little dresses.

Catherine thought of her lonely childhood and remembered how she had longed to have a brother or a sister, but when Papa was killed in an accident, her mother had never remarried. Joey would have the playmate she never had.

A smile came to Catherine's face as she thought of her little ones playing together.

Mama and Charlie arrived early in the morning for a visit.

"Too wet to work in the fields," Mama said.

"Yes, it's a great time for a visit, come let's sit on the porch and I will tell you all about the twister that passed over us," Catherine said.

"Why don't we go see your garden and pick some beans, then while we sit, I will help you snap them," Mama answered.

"Oh, Mama, you are so organized," Catherine laughed, "but it will help us to get an early start on supper."

The long slender beans soon filled their basket and they returned to the shade of the porch to snap them.

"How are you feeling, Catherine?" Mama asked.

"I've had morning sickness and I have been throwing up, but it's getting better. I'm with child, Mama," Catherine announced.

"I figured that out. James came to talk to me, he was so worried about you." Mama told her.

"I'm sorry James was worried. I was going to tell him soon. At first, I was so overwhelmed by everything and I wasn't very happy; but now I'm better and I'm very glad we are going to have another child. Joey will be delighted when he finds out we will have a new baby by Christmas time," Catherine said.

"We are all excited, Catherine, and we hope Daniel and Billie will be home by Christmas," Mama replied.

"I must write to Daniel. I will send it to Atlanta. He might still be there; if not, perhaps they would send it on to wherever he has gone."

"Yes, Daniel would want to know about the child," Mama said.

Mama and Charlie stayed all day. It was good for Rachel and Jacob to have the time alone at home, Mama thought.

The boys enjoyed being together. James took Charlie and Joey to the creek to fish and Mama and Catherine cooked supper.

"This has been so good, Mama. We really needed this time together and to have a rest from cotton chopping," Catherine said.

Mama set the table while Catherine dished up the buttered green beans, deviled eggs, and fresh baked corn bread with a basket of spring plums for dessert.

James poked his head in the kitchen door.

"Is supper ready?" he called.

"No," Mama said, "we're waiting for the fish."

"You're out of luck, we didn't catch any fish. The creek is too high from all the rain," James replied.

"No, you're out of luck, no supper now," Mama teased.

The boys were hungry and soon consumed all the supper.

These plums are so sweet," Mama said, "where did you pick them?"

"From the thicket, by the big oak tree," James said.

"Can we stop and pick some, Mama?" Charlie asked.

"We will have to get going now if we are going to stop, but yes we will stop and gather some," Mama answered.

Catherine waved good-bye as the buggy disappeared down the lane. Tomorrow the cotton chopping would start again.

Chapter 13

The Stranger Received

A sturdy boy romped through the woods, searching for hickory nuts and black walnuts. He carried a flour sack over his shoulder. His blond hair lay in wispy, sun-streaked waves over his forehead, tousled by the wind. He stopped dead in his tracks as he came near the spring; some one was beside the spring!

Slowly the boy approached the spring, he could now see that the man lying by the spring was a confederate soldier. He must be dead, the boy thought, he's so still.

Daniel groaned and rolled over. He looked up into the startled blue eyes of a boy about 10 years old.

The boy stood frozen, Daniel could see the fear in his eyes. "Hello, son, could you help me?" he asked.

"Who are you?" the boy asked.

"I'm Daniel Woodall from Warm Springs, Georgia. I was fighting the union army with General Hood's army, but we couldn't stop them. We had to retreat and I was separated from my regiment. I'm not sure how long I have been here. I'm so weak because I haven't eaten in days," Daniel replied.

"I have some buttered corn bread and an apple," the boy said.

Opening the bag, he pulled out the bread and handed it to Daniel.

Daniel ate the bread slowly, it tasted so good. When he finished the bread the boy handed him the apple.

"No, you need to eat too," Daniel said.

"Oh, I'm not hungry, I just left home a while ago, go ahead and eat the apple," he said.

The apple was sweet and juicy and Daniel ate just about everything except the seeds.

"How far away is your home?" Daniel asked.

"Not far, just down that path until you come to the road and around the bend is our house," the boy answered.

"Do you think I could come home with you until I'm strong enough to travel? Perhaps you could go ask your Papa," Daniel requested.

The boy shook his head. "No, I can't ask my Pa, he's been gone a long time and my grandpa, too, but I'm sure Mama and Grandma will give you some supper. Come on, I'll help you stand up."

Sticking out his hand, the boy said, "I'm Lucas Lee. Welcome to Winchester, Tennessee."

Smiling, Daniel grasped his hand, using his gun as a crutch; he stood and said, "Thank you, Luke."

Daniels head cleared as he followed Luke down the narrow path.

The December sun was warm on Daniel's back as he and Luke walked slowly along the road. The late Indian summer weather was pleasant and the golden brown leaves drifted from the trees to the road.

Around the bend was a small frame house. The porch was covered with morning glory vines still green and pretty, which was unusual for this time of year. Lambs' ears grew in a neat row around the porch and some perennials still bloomed in the yard.

"The Morning Glories are still pretty for so late in the fall," Daniel said.

"Oh, Grandma covers them when it frosts, she hates when the cold comes and kills them. They are a sight in the morning with all those big blue flowers. Grandma loves her flowers. She says God gave us flowers to nourish our souls. I guess she means when you sit quiet on the swing and see the beauty of the flowers you feel God's Spirit. Sometimes I like to do that," he said.

Dashing up the steps, Luke called to the young woman standing in the doorway, "Mama, I found this soldier by the spring. He is lost and hungry. Can you and Grandma give him some supper?"

An older woman appeared behind the young woman and slowly they came to the edge of the porch.

Daniel stood at the bottom of the steps, leaning on his gun. He was sure he was a frightening sight to the women.

Lifting his cap, he said, "Hello, I am Daniel Woodall. I was fighting with General Hood's army, there were so many Yankees we could not stop them. We were told to retreat and every man ran for his life. I have been lying by the spring in the woods. Luke found me there and gave me his lunch. I had not eaten for a long time, and I'm very hungry. Could you spare any food that I can regain my strength and try to find my way back to the army?"

The older woman came down the steps, she extended her hand to Daniel. He looked with wonder at the woman, though she was older her face seemed regal and a soft glow seemed to come from her. She spoke with a musical lilt. "Welcome to our home, Daniel. I am Marion Culpepper, wife of Jacob, and this is my daughter, Rebecca Lee. Our food is limited, but we will share all that we have. It looks as though you could use a bath and a rest."

Turning to Luke, Marion said, "Build a fire under the wash pot and fill it, get the water nice and hot and fill the bath tub in the wash shed."

"Rebecca, bring some of Nathaniel's clothes for Daniel," Marion continued.

"By the time your bath is finished, Daniel, we will have supper ready. Hurry, Luke, it looks like he will fall over soon," Marion called.

"Rebecca, bring a plate of buttered corn bread and a glass of milk to keep Daniel going until we can get some real food into him."

Daniel sat in the hot soapy water and thanked God for bringing him to this kind, caring family. He dressed in Nathaniel's clothes even though they were big on him.

The dirty, ragged uniform was dropped into the soapy water to soak. Daniel would finish washing it after supper.

Daniel pulled on his worn boots over the clean socks Rebecca had furnished. He combed his hair and shaved with the razor he carried in his pocket.

The warm tantalizing smell of pinto beans and ham hocks floated from the kitchen along with the wonderful smell of cooking apples.

"Come in, Daniel," Marion called, "Supper is almost ready."

"My, don't you look like a new man," Luke said.

Rebecca pulled out the chair at the head of the table. "Mama said to seat you here."

Marion brought four steaming bowls of beans and ham to the table. Hot corn bread and chunky applesauce sat in the middle of the table. Luke poured milk from the canister that came from the well.

"Daniel, would you bless our food?" Marion asked.

Daniel bowed his head and prayed God's blessing upon the household and the food. Never had he eaten anything that tasted so good as that supper.

The early rays of Indian summer sun filtered into the washhouse. Daniel rolled over; his first thought was "I feel so good, where am I?" Then he remembered coming to Marion's house, the bath, the food and the bed Luke had prepared for him.

Luke had stuffed the cotton sacks with hay, laying them out side by side, making a large bed. Marion had covered them with blankets and a feather quilt. Daniel had slept soundly, no hunger, no bullets, and no screams of the dying.

Thoughts of Catherine came to him, what had happened in her life since he left her in March. He had heard nothing in all these months. Joey would be talking very well by now and growing so big.

Daniel prayed for all his family and Charlie and Garth. He wondered if they were both still alive. He had seen so many young men die and he wondered why he still lived when so many had died. He remembered the words Catherine had spoken long ago, "God has a plan, Daniel, and we are living out that plan."

A small, blonde head appeared around the wash shed door. "Are you awake, Daniel?" Luke called.

"Yes, come in, Luke. I've been awake since dawn. What are you doing up so early?" Daniel asked.

"Oh, I always get up early. Sometimes I go do my chores before breakfast so I have time to go play in the woods," Luke replied.

"That reminds me, you never got to gather your hickory nuts and walnuts yesterday. Maybe I could help you do that today," Daniel said.

Luke's face beamed his approval as he answered, "I would really like that."

"Grandma said to tell you breakfast will be ready soon," Luke said as he disappeared out the door.

Luke sat at the table watching his Grandma cook. "I like Daniel. I wish he would stay with us for a while. He said he would help me look for hickory nuts and walnuts today. Maybe he could fix the leaking roof you and Mama have been so worried about. I'll bet Daniel can do about anything," Luke said.

Marion smiled at her young grandson. She could understand how lonesome he was for male companionship since his Papa and Grandfather had gone to war.

"Perhaps Daniel will stay a while, we must wait and see what he feels he must do," Marion said.

Daniel appeared at the kitchen door. "Come in, Daniel, breakfast is almost ready. Luke, run get your mother, she is building a fire under the wash pot to heat water for washing clothes."

Luke scampered away to find Rebecca and Daniel stood by the table.

"Sit down, here at the head of the table. It's comforting to have a man at the head of the table."

Daniel's eyes followed Marion. What was it that seemed to radiate from her? She seemed so serene in the midst of all her work and concern.

Placing a large bowl of cornmeal mush on the table, Marion added the syrup and milk, stirring the mixture.

Rebecca placed the flat iron on the hot stove and sat down.

"Mush again, Grandma," Luke said.

"You know today is mush day," Marion answered.

"I know, but I thought since we have company we might have eggs two times this week."

"You know, Luke, this mush looks wonderful to me. Let's bless it and eat it up so we can do some fun thing today," Daniel said.

Luke grinned at Daniel and said, "Yeah, today we're going to find lots of nuts."

"Could we take time for a talk, Daniel, after breakfast?" Marion asked.

"Of course, Miss Marion," Daniel answered.

"Luke, help your mother with the dishes while Daniel and I talk," Marion said.

"Come, Daniel, let's sit on the swing. I know you have to go back to the army, but does it have to be right away. Rebecca and I have been praying about several things. You might be the answer to our prayers."

"I am so grateful for your hospitality that I will do anything I can to help you. I probably would have died there by the spring if Luke hadn't happened along."

Marion smiled a sweet smile. "Thank you, Daniel," she said.

"It's time to butcher the pigs for our winter meat, but Rebecca and I have no way to kill them. Last year old Mr. Johnson came and helped us, but he died in January. We prayed God would help us find a way to butcher the pigs and you arrived with a gun. We also need to fix the roof. We have the needed materials but neither of us know the first thing about fixing the roof," Marion said.

"I will help you with the butchering and I will fix the roof before I leave," Daniel said.

"I'm not sure what to do, I have no way to know where my unit went if any of them survived. Perhaps the union army killed them all, so many had already died. When they said retreat, I just ran away as fast as I could," Daniel continued.

"God will show you what to do. Now, go and enjoy your day with Luke. He is so excited to have you here," Marion said.

"Okay, Luke, which way do we go?" Daniel asked.

"We will go back to the spring, there is a big walnut tree nearby. That's where I was headed when I found you. Not too far away is a grove of hickory trees." Luke said.

Luke was so excited he ran ahead to the walnut tree.

"Come on, Daniel, look at all the walnuts. It's a bumper crop."

They filled Luke's bag with walnuts. "We will leave your bag here and pick it up on our way home," Daniel said.

"Now, let's see what else we can find to fill up my bag." The path ran around some huge oak trees. Daniel stopped and raked away the leaves and, sure enough, he found what he was looking for—a patch of Sheep Head mushrooms. "Have you ever eaten these?" Daniel asked.

"No, I never have. Are you sure they are good to eat?" Luke asked, doubtfully.

Daniel laughed, "They taste almost like steak, fried with some green marsh onions. You'll love them."

"It's late to find Sheep Heads, must be the warm weather," Daniel said.

They carefully cut and placed all the mushrooms in Daniel's bag. It made Daniel hungry just thinking about how good they would taste.

When they reached the hickory trees, they found many nuts on the ground. They removed the mushrooms and filled the bag with nuts, placing the mushrooms back in the top of the bag.

"Now let's go back to the spring and see if we can find a wild onion patch in the damp soil," Daniel said.

Sure enough, they found the onions.

Luke was so excited to take home two bags of food.

He ran up the steps, calling, "Mama, Grandma, come and see all the food Daniel and I found."

Marion greeted them with a smile as they unloaded the mushrooms and onions.

"Where did you ever find the Sheep Heads, we haven't had them in years," Marion cried.

"The cold will get them soon, but they grow so quickly we might get another picking in a few days." Daniel said.

Marion served bean soup for lunch and promised they would have fried mushrooms for supper.

The first day at Marion's house passed in peace and harmony, the morning with Luke had been fun making Daniel think of the days to come with Joey. In the afternoon, they worked together bringing all the roof supplies to the porch. Tomorrow they would fix the roof.

Daniel and Luke took over the barn chores. Rebecca was so grateful to have a break. She came from the house to take the milk.

Daniel noticed the sad look in Rebecca's eyes and knew how much she longed for Nathaniel to return.

Luke went to close the pasture gate and Rebecca asked Daniel, "What is war like?"

Daniel saw sadness in her eyes and a deep concern for Nathaniel. He could feel Catherine's concern for him reflected in Rebecca's feelings.

"War is awful, Rebecca, you watch so many people die and you almost wish you would die also so you wouldn't have to watch the suffering anymore. But, when you have a family that loves you and prays for you, it helps to keep you going. I don't think the war will last much longer. Nathaniel and Jacob will come home soon, we hope," Daniel replied.

"I pray every day for the war to end so Nathaniel and Pa can come home," Becky replied.

Daniel and Luke fixed the roof and sealed around the chimney. The first rainy day would tell if they had fixed the leak.

"We must winterize the wash shed," Marion said, "because the cold rains will come soon and we don't want you shivering out here in the shed."

Daniel and Luke chinked all the cracks with red mud clay, stopping up all the cracks where cold air could come in.

A slow, steady rain began one week after Daniel arrived at Marion's house. The temperature dropped and in the morning a thin layer of ice coated Daniel's washbasin. The goose down quilt had kept Daniel so snug and warm through the night that he was surprised how cold the morning was.

Luke's knock announced breakfast and he and Daniel arrived in the warm kitchen.

Marion served fried eggs, grits and buttered biscuits with molasses.

"Grandma, you made my favorite breakfast," Luke exclaimed.

"I think we should butcher the hogs tomorrow," Daniel announced.

Chapter 14

Butchering, Christmas and Surprises

Butchering Day was a busy day for everyone. Luke carried firewood to build the fire under the scalding tub. Then he began to fill the tubs with water. Becky lit the fire and helped finish carrying the water.

Daniel killed the two fat hogs and used a horse to drag them to the tub. Then everyone worked together to scrape and clean the hair from the hogs.

Daniel cut the meat while Becky and Marion washed and dried the hams and slabs of bacon. Then all the meat was packed into the saltbox and covered in salt, except the fresh pork they kept to grind into sausage and the fat they would render into lard.

After the meat was salt cured, it would be removed from the box, washed thoroughly and hung in the smoke house. A slow-burning fire would be built in the fire pit with apple and hickory wood, and then the meat would be cured with a delicious flavor, providing meat for the family.

"What would we have done if God had not sent you to help us, Daniel?" Marion asked.

Daniel was glad the days were so busy. It didn't leave much time to think about Catherine and home. His heart ached when he thought of them and he thanked God again that James and Rachel's Jacob would be there to help Catherine with her butchering.

Every night Daniel prayed for guidance, asking God to show him what to do. He did not know where the union army was, nor the confederate army. The thought of being captured by the union army was frightening. Daniel remembered the sadness of Charlie being captured and prayed for him and Garth. He longed to write to Catherine, but the union army had blown up all the railroad tracks, so no mail could be sent.

The day after butchering was chilly with a brisk wind. Daniel and Luke did all the barn chores after breakfast. Rebecca was so happy to be relieved of barn work and wood chopping, it had been such a big job for her and Luke, but for Daniel it seemed so easy. Luke was so different now that Daniel had come.

Rebecca hummed softly as she set the table for dinner. She brought Mama's pretty dishes from the cupboard. The dishes had been a wedding present to Mama and Papa. She traced the delicate pattern of tiny pink roses with her finger and remembered all the happy occasions they had celebrated using these dishes. Mama always told her that some day they would belong to her.

The table was beautiful and this would be a special meal. Marion had cooked fresh sausage and made corn bread dressing with sliced, boiled eggs and chopped green marsh onions mixed in the dressing. A dish of winter squash and baked apples completed the meal.

Daniel sat at the head of the table, Marion and Becky on the sides and Luke at the other end.

Marion read Psalm 100 from the family Bible. Daniel blessed their food and prayed for Nathaniel and Jacob, asking God to provide them with food. He prayed for Catherine and Mama and tears came as he pictured them around Mama's big kitchen table praying for him and Papa.

The December days slipped away as Daniel and Luke did barn chores, cut firewood and hunted for food. They cracked and shelled all the walnuts and hickory nuts they had picked.

Christmas was coming and Daniel wanted to make something special for Luke, but he could think of nothing. He knew what he would make for Marion and Rebecca.

A sudden movement in the woodpile caught Daniel's eye. What was hiding there? Moving the sticks of firewood carefully aside, he uncovered a small raccoon. He covered the raccoon with his jacket and lifted it up.

An idea popped into Daniel's mind. He had heard that raccoons made wonderful pets, almost as good as a puppy, Daniel thought. He went to the barn and placed the raccoon in a chicken crate. He would enlist Marion to help him with small scraps of food; by Christmas time, she would be tame. The raccoon would be a companion for Luke, when he was gone.

Daniel knew that he must go back to war, but he truly didn't know where to go. Marion had heard in Winchester that Atlanta was being rebuilt by the people returning to their homes. Perhaps he should return to Atlanta and see what was happening there. He knew his chances of finding Papa were very slim.

Every weekday morning Luke had lessons for two hours. Rebecca was working with him on reading and arithmetic. The school in Winchester had been closed for a long time. The teacher had been sent to war. While Luke did his lessons, Daniel trained the little raccoon. She was growing fast with the steady diet of chopped apples, bread scraps and milk. He hid her crate in the hayloft and, so far, Luke had not discovered it.

"Come on, Luke, let's go look for a Christmas tree," Daniel called as Luke entered the barn.

Running back to the house, Luke called to Rebecca, "We're going for the Christmas tree. Will you and Grandma get the tree holder and the decorations ready?"

"Yes, Luke, we will be ready and we'll decorate the tree after supper," Rebecca answered.

A cold wind blew as Daniel and Luke crossed the field and entered the woods. They looked at many trees, but could not find a good one. Finally, they found a nicely shaped cedar tree. Daniel chopped the small tree down and he and Luke pulled it home.

Luke was unusually quiet on the way home.

He looked up at Daniel and asked, "Do you think my Papa is dead?"

Dropping the tree, Daniel knelt down and gathered Luke in his arms. "Oh, Luke, we hope and pray your Papa will return when the war is over and your grandpa, too."

Luke laid his head on Daniel's shoulder and swiped away tears with his fist. "I'm so glad you came, Daniel, and I found you by the spring," he whispered.

Marion made popcorn for Luke and Daniel to eat and string. Daniel pushed the needle through and Luke pulled the corn to the end of the long thread. They laughed and sang Christmas songs as they made garlands of popcorn for the Christmas tree. Marion placed a beautiful gold star on the top of the tree and Rebecca tied on the ornaments.

Marion brought the special Christmas candle that had belonged to her mother. When the candle was lit it was officially Christmas Eve.

Luke liked to read from the Bible, especially from the book that carried his name. He read the Christmas story from the book of Luke.

Daniel awakened early on Christmas Day. A cold, aching pain lay in his chest. Would he ever go home to Catherine and Joey? He prayed for his loved ones and thank God for this safe time with Marion's family. He opened the wash shed door and looked out on a chilly, blustery Christmas day.

The Christmas gifts were all arranged on the back porch, the chicken crate covered with a horse blanket.

"Hurry, Daniel, breakfast is almost ready," Luke called from the doorway. "As soon as we eat, we can open our presents."

"I'm coming, Luke, and I'm hungry. Breakfast sure smells good."

Marion prayed before breakfast, "Lord God, thank you for this food you have provided for us this day. We pray that Jacob and Nathaniel are safe and have food today. Bless Daniel's family, Lord, and provide for their needs while Daniel is away. We pray the war will soon end and families can be reunited. Thank you for the gift of Jesus, Our Lord, on this Christmas day. Amen."

Luke was anxious for Daniel to open his gift. "I helped Mama and Grandma make your present," he exclaimed.

Daniel pulled the gift from the wrapping, soft knitted wool gloves and matching scarf.

"I helped Mama make the wool thread on the spinning wheel," Luke said.

Pulling on the gloves, Daniel said, "They fit perfect and will be so warm when I am traveling. Thank you all for such a thoughtful gift."

"Now I have presents for all of you." Going to the porch, Daniel brought new clothes poles for Marion's clothesline.

"Oh, Daniel, you knew what I needed," Marion laughed.

Rebecca loved the willow stool Daniel had made for her.

"Now, Luke, you sit on the stool and close your eyes while I get your gift," Daniel said.

"What is it, Daniel, and where do you have to go for my gift?" Luke asked.

"I'll just be a minute, now close your eyes."

"Okay, I'm back. Open your eyes," Daniel said softly.

Luke stared at the crate.

"Go ahead, uncover it." Daniel said.

Slowly, Luke pulled the blanket from the crate and the little raccoon stared out at him. "A pet, I always wanted a pet," Luke said. "Will it bite?"

Daniel laughed as he pulled the raccoon from the crate.

"She is as gentle as can be and she will be your constant companion. She will love you as much as you love her."

"What will you name her?" Daniel asked.

"I don't know. I have to think about a special name." Luke said.

The little raccoon curled up in Luke's lap when he sat down and he stroked her fur.

Daniel, Luke and the raccoon went to do the barn chores and milk the cow. The raccoon followed everywhere they went. Luke scooped her up when the cow almost stepped on her.

"You better watch out, Little Missy, or you will get squished," he said.

"Little Missy?" asked Daniel.

"Yes, that's her name," Luke grinned.

Luke carried the milk and Missy and Daniel brought a set of horse hanes as they returned to the house. The hanes were worn and almost broken. He would repair them for Marion.

It was almost dark when Daniel and Marion heard a horse coming. "Who would be coming so late in the day?" Marion wondered. Fear flashed in her eyes as she looked at Daniel.

Daniel went to the window and looked out. A young man was lifting an older man from a small mule.

"Someone is hurt," Daniel said. "I must go help."

Marion came to the window and cried, "O my God, my dear God, Jacob and Nathaniel have returned from the war."

Marion, Rebecca and Luke rushed from the house. They embraced their family crying.

"Jacob is hurt, we must get him into the house," Nathaniel said.

"Hello, Nathaniel. I am a soldier that Rebecca and Marion have befriended. Let me carry Jacob," Daniel said.

Jacob was so thin and frail. Daniel carried him gently.

"Quick, Luke, place a chair by the stove and cover it with a quilt. Marion, heat some milk and get it into Jacob," Daniel said.

Nathaniel leaned against the closed door with Rebecca supporting him. He looked as though he would collapse at any minute.

"We have traveled a long way. We wanted to be home for Christmas," Nathaniel said.

The food was heated and supper was served with great joy and thanksgiving.

Daniel closed the kitchen door softly as he slipped away. He took the little mule to the barn and fed and watered him. "Thank you, little mule, for bringing such a wonderful Christmas miracle to this family," Daniel thought.

Tomorrow, Daniel would talk with Nathaniel. "Was the war over?" he wondered. A great longing swept over him to go home to Catherine and Joey.

Luke's head popped in the wash shed door. "Grandma wants to know what's keeping you, Daniel. Breakfast is ready, come on," he called.

Daniel had lingered in his little place because things were different now that Nathaniel and Jacob had returned. He didn't want to intrude.

Daniel followed Luke to the kitchen.

The stool Daniel had made and a bench from Marion's room provided a seat for everyone.

"Come, Daniel, sit here by me so we can talk," Jacob said.

Marion and Rebecca had made a wonderful homecoming breakfast of scrambled eggs, sausage and cornmeal muffins.

"We will have to eat mush all the rest of the week, but today we celebrate," Rebecca said.

They held hands around the table and Jacob prayed a prayer of thanksgiving.

"Marion tells me you have been a great blessing, Daniel. Thank you for helping our family," Jacob said.

"Is the war over, Jacob?" Daniel asked.

"I really don't know. Nathaniel found me in an entrenchment in pursuit of Sherman. I was bleeding from a bayonet wound and probably would have died. He ripped a dead soldiers shirt and put a tourniquet on my leg and got the bleeding stopped. The confederate soldiers were retreating and I would have been left behind, but Nathaniel drug me into the deep woods and covered me with brush. The union army passed just yards away from where I lay. Late that night, Nathaniel returned with a little food and water and the mule. He said we are going home. We hid in the woods during the day and traveled mostly at night. One family hid us for three weeks because there were so many union soldiers around we didn't dare try to travel. I'm sure the angels of the Lord brought us through. I couldn't see them, but I could feel their presence," Jacob said.

"Sherman has killed, burned and looted his way across Georgia and he's probably in Charleston by now. The south can't possibly win this war; our only hope is that Lee will surrender. I figured God intended me to find Pa, when I saw him I knew what I was going to do. We had fought for the confederacy long enough," Nathaniel said.

"It's a miracle you are here," Marion said.

Nathaniel, Luke and Daniel finished breakfast and went to the barn.

"Do you think I could get home without being captured by the union army?" Daniel asked.

"Well, Daniel, I think you can get to Atlanta, but you won't find much there. The main part of the city is just a charred mess. Pa and I stayed there for a while with some families that are rebuilding their homes. There were no union soldiers there, but there were some confederate soldiers. They seem to be looking out for the civilians that are returning," Nathaniel answered.

"I think I should try to get back to Atlanta," Daniel said.

Nathaniel fed and watered the mule. "His name is Moses, I named him Moses because he was our deliverer. Without him, I couldn't have brought Pa home," he said.

"When you go you may have Moses, he was part of God's plan to get Pa and I home. Perhaps he will be part of His plan to get you home also," Nathaniel whispered with tears in his eyes.

"Thank you, Nathaniel, Moses is a wonderful gift and I accept him with renewed hope. I believe I will get home to Catherine and Joey," Daniel answered.

"I must talk with Jacob and Marion and make plans to start my journey," Daniel said.

"I'll miss you, Daniel, and you know I love you," Luke said sadly.

Little Missy climbed on Luke's shoulder while he sat on Daniel's bed watching him pack his few belongings.

Daniel stopped and sat down beside Luke. "You will always be a part of me, Luke, because you saved my life, but I must go home to my family."

"I know," Luke sighed, "but I'll still miss you."

Daniel looked around the simple shed where he had been warm and comfortable. He thanked God for his care and the time he had spent at Marion's home.

Moses stood waiting in the early morning light, frost covered the ground. Nathaniel had folded and tied the warm feather quilt that Marion had insisted Daniel take. It made a fine saddle and would keep him warm at night. A small bag of grain and a flour sack filled with food were tied behind the quilt.

All the family gathered to bid Daniel good-bye.

"Godspeed, my son. Thank you for helping my family," Jacob said.

Nathaniel gave Daniel a big bear hug and said, "Now take good care of Moses."

Rebecca hugged Daniel and thanked him for all the chores he had done for her.

"Good-bye, Daniel, you have truly been a blessing and like a son. When all the world is sane again, write to us and let us know how you made it home," Marion said.

Daniel lifted Luke into his arms. "Good-bye, my friend, you are a fine boy and I'm so glad you found me," Daniel said.

"I love you and I'll miss you," Luke replied.

Daniel rode out of sight and Marion said, "He is a good man and we were blessed that he came. God will bring good to him."

Chapter 15

The Long Summer

Catherine moved slowly through the garden, she was heavy with child. Joey chattered as he followed behind her. They reached the dry potato vines and Catherine knelt down to dig the potatoes. Joey helped her dig with a large spoon. The basket was soon filled. They filled another basket with beans and okra. Catherine carried the baskets from the garden and returned for Joey.

Mama, James and Charlie were in the field picking cotton. They had decided that Catherine would not go to the field anymore. She was too heavy to bend and crawl. She would stay home, care for Joey and prepare the meals.

The beans dropped into the basket as Catherine sat snapping them in a steady rhythm. She prayed for Daniel as she snapped. She had not heard from him since he kissed her good-bye and said "See you soon, my love," and she had replied "I'll be waiting." She no longer cried. She simply waited and hoped that he was alive.

Supper was ready. Catherine washed Joey's face and hands and waited for Mama and the boys. They arrived, tired and dusty.

Conversation was slow.

Mama said, "Supper is delicious, Catherine. We hate to eat and run, but we need to get home and help Rachel with the chores, as I'm sure Jacob is still working in our fields. It's amazing how much cotton he can pick with only one hand."

James went to the barn to milk and feed the animals. Catherine began to stack the dishes; another lonely day without Daniel was almost completed. The baby kicked, she laid her hand over the movement and prayed.

The leaves began to turn with the first light frost. The cotton picking was finished. James had taken the cotton to the gin. No buyer had come from Atlanta to buy the local cotton; most of the railroads had been destroyed by the union army. James received no money for the cotton, only the promise that when a buyer came he would receive his money.

Catherine leaned against the house. She had been washing clothes since early morning. Gazing up into the late October sky, she wondered where Daniel was at this moment.

They had heard that Atlanta now belonged to the union army, led by General Sherman.

"Oh, God, wherever Daniel is at this time, send your guarding angels to keep him safe," Catherine prayed.

Catherine rolled over in bed; a burning pain ran down her spine and into her legs. She sat up in bed waiting for the pain to subdue; perhaps she had done too much yesterday when they butchered the hogs.

The pain continued in Catherine's back. By afternoon, she had returned to bed because she could not bear the pain.

Catherine called from her bed, "James, take Joey in the wagon and go for Mama."

Mama arrived in the buggy to take Catherine to see Dr. Hayes in Warm Springs.

"What do you think is wrong, Mama?" Catherine asked.

"I'm not sure what's wrong, dear, but I want you to be near Dr. Hayes if anything is wrong."

"James, take a quilt and pillows to the buggy then come and help me get Catherine in the buggy," Mama said.

Kissing the boys good-bye, they quickly rolled away down the lane.

Catherine lay with her eyes closed, breathing deeply. It seemed to help control the pain.

The buggy ride was smooth. Catherine was grateful she didn't have to go in the wagon.

Reaching over to hold Mama's hand, Catherine said, "Mama, please pray for the baby to be safe."

Mama stopped the mare and took Catherine's hands in hers. "Yes, Catherine, let's ask God to watch over you and the baby," she said.

Catherine felt better as the buggy rolled on. Now it was committed to God and she must leave her little one in His hands.

Dr. Hayes helped Catherine into bed, listening carefully as she told him about the pain.

"I think you did too much lifting yesterday. You need bed rest for several days. I suggest you stay here so I can be close if anything develops. We hope the baby is not coming yet, it will be six weeks early," he said.

Catherine looked at the doctor with sad eyes. "I have Joey to care for Dr. Hayes. I can't stay here," she cried.

Mama said, "Rachel and I will take care of Joey. He will be just fine. I think you should stay here with Dr. Hayes and his wife. The rest will be good for you."

Tears gathered in Catherine's eyes and she agreed she would stay until the pain went away.

Mama hugged Catherine, "I will be praying for you and the baby, Catherine. Try to rest and don't worry about Joey," she said.

As the door closed, a deep loneliness settled over Catherine. The medicine Dr. Hayes had given her began to take effect and she drifted off to sleep thinking of Daniel.

Severe pain awakened Catherine. Something was very wrong. Pulling the cord that would ring a bell in the doctor's bedroom, Catherine waited.

Dr. and Mrs. Hayes appeared in a flurry.

"What's wrong, Catherine?" Dr. Hayes asked.

"The pain is very bad," Catherine gasped.

Turning to his wife, Dr. Hayes said, "Stir up the fire and boil some water. I think she is going into labor."

"Oh, Dr. Hayes, it's too soon," Catherine said.

"Well, dear, we must do what we can and ask God to help us," he replied.

Mrs. Hayes hurried away to the kitchen and Catherine moaned as another pain burned through her.

Daylight filtered through the window. Dr. Hayes opened the office door and called out to a passing man, "Please take a message to the livery stable. Ask the owner to send one of his boys to Elizabeth Woodall's farm and tell her to come to my office right away."

"Yes, sir," the man said and sped away to the stable.

Catherine cried out in anguish as the pain surged through her. She knew they were labor pains and prayed God would watch over her baby.

The clock ticked slowly and Catherine's eyes followed the passing of time. She thought she would surely die. The pain was so awful.

Mama arrived.

"Oh, Catherine, I came as fast as I could. Hold on, dear, it won't be much longer," Mama said.

"What's happening, Dr. Hayes?" Mama asked.

"It's too soon for the baby to be born, Elizabeth, but we must do what we can to deliver this baby and take care of Catherine. She is our major concern right now," he said.

"Relax, Catherine, when the pain goes; then, push with all your might when the pain returns."

The hands on the clock moved slowly to 12:00 noon. Catherine was consumed with pain.

"Good, Catherine, keep pushing. The head is coming, the baby is small, next pain push out the shoulders," Dr. Hayes coached.

As the next pain came, Catherine pushed with all her might and the baby was born. She waited for the cry as Dr. Hayes cut the cord and worked over the baby. There was no cry. Slowly Catherine drifted away into darkness.

"Wake up, Catherine," Mama whispered.

Slowly Catherine's eyes focused on Mama's tear-stained face and she knew the baby was dead.

"The baby was born dead, a little boy. He only weighed five pounds. Dr. Hayes wants you to see him. He has washed him and wrapped him in a blanket. He will bring him to you now," Mama said.

Catherine's heart felt like a heavy stone. Joey's little brother would never run and play and call her "Mama" and Daniel would never see him.

Dr. Hayes laid the tiny bundle in Catherine's outstretched arms. He closed the door and left her alone.

Catherine looked at the precious little face. He looked like Joey. Clutching him to her breast, she sobbed into the blanket.

"Oh, God, why?" she cried aloud.

Mama returned and gently lifted the infant from Catherine's arms.

"There will be other children, Catherine, when Daniel returns, but we will always miss this precious little one."

James straightened up and looked toward the church. Mama, Rachel, Jacob and Charlie were coming with Rev. Roper. The grave was dug and James lifted the tiny casket from the buggy. Catherine's baby boy was buried in the Primitive Baptist Church Cemetery.

Chapter 16

Christmas in Warm Springs

Catherine sat rocking Joey. He had been sleeping for sometime. James had offered to put him in bed, but Catherine needed to hold Joey. Holding him helped to push away the sad, gray life that had enveloped her since the baby died. She tried to hide the depression from James, but James was so aware that there was no longer a sparkle in her eyes. No laughter came from her lips. It seemed as though part of Catherine's heart had been buried with the tiny baby.

"Let me put Joey to bed now," James said.

Lifting Joey from Catherine's lap, James tucked him into his bed and returned to the kitchen to talk.

"Will we put up a Christmas tree this year?" James asked.

"Yes, we will have a Christmas tree. Do you have one picked out?" Catherine replied.

"Yes, a pretty little pine not far from the house." James answered.

"Remember the holly tree with the red berries you found last year," Catherine said.

James nodded," It was a special tree. You don't find them very often."

"I have no gifts for you or Joey and I'm so sorry," Catherine sighed.

"Please don't worry about gifts. God's gift of Jesus is all our gift and we have each other. I have made gifts for Joey. I've whittled more pieces for his farm. I made a farmhouse and people and a dog and a cat."

"Thank you so much for remembering Joey," Catherine said.

"I must cook something special for Christmas dinner. Maybe, I'll make a black walnut pie. I'll bet it would be almost as good as pecan pie," Catherine said.

James laughed, "I'll crack the walnuts tomorrow and we will make a black walnut pie. We have molasses and eggs to go into the pie.

James smiled at Catherine. She had been sad for so long, he hoped she would begin to heal inside and find peace over the loss of the baby. He prayed for the old Catherine to return.

The next day, James took the wagon and went to see Mama. He needed some advice about a gift he had made for Catherine. Before the baby died, he had fashioned a beautiful little cradle from small willow limbs. Then he had carved a tiny little baby from the soft white willow wood. He did not know if he should give her the gift or hide it away.

"It's so good to see you, James. Give me your coat and sit down. I will fix you a mug of hot sausage soup," Mama said.

"I've worked for a long time on a gift for Catherine. I started it way back in the summer. It was almost complete when the baby died. Now I don't know if I should give it to her. She is still so sad and depressed," James said.

Mama sat, thinking. Then she answered, "Carve in memory and the date the baby died on the bottom. Catherine needs to put this behind her, but that is not easy to do. Perhaps if she knows we will always remember, she will begin to heal. Only God can take away the pain of losing a child."

Charlie hurried into the kitchen dropping his load of wood into the wood box.

"When do you think they will be here, Mama," Charlie asked.

"Pretty soon," Mama answered.

"Will we open gifts as soon as they arrive?" Charlie questioned.

"Yes, if Rachel has her gifts ready. I'm ready," Mama said.

"I can't wait to give Joey his gifts," Charlie said.

He and Rachel had worked for days making special gifts for Joey. Rachel had embroidered faces on a clown and a little monkey they had made from one of Papa's socks. Charlie had gathered all the left over cotton he could find and stuffed them. They had also made a wooly brown dog.

Mama had worked for months on her gifts. She had pieced together a little brown donkey with a cart in the center of a beautiful quilt.

The Christmas tree stood in the living room all decorated, with the gifts underneath. The smell of ham drifted from the kitchen. A blazing fire crackled in the fireplace. Mama stood by the fire thinking of other Christmases. She prayed for Papa and Daniel, asking God to end the war and bring them home.

The sound of the approaching wagon brought Charlie to the front door.

"Merry Christmas," he called.

Catherine stood looking into the big, cheerful room, the glowing fire, the lovely tree and Mama's smiling face. It was almost like before the war. She walked slowly to the tree and placed her gifts there. Last night, she had taken out the box that contained what things she had that had belonged to her parents: Papa's gold pocket watch, given to James; Mama's beautiful gold necklace and earrings would now belong to this Mama and Rachel; Papa's two pocket knives, one for Charlie and one for Jacob.

"Come on, Joey, open your presents," Charlie said.

Clapping his hands in excitement, Joey plopped to the floor ready for the presents. He unrolled the quilt and out came the clown, the monkey and a wooly brown dog.

Joey patted the little donkey on his quilt and said, "Thank you, Grandma."

The gifts were given with love and tears. When Catherine opened her gift from James, she burst into tears and threw her arms around him.

"Thank you, thank you, James, now Daniel can know when he returns."

The tears unlocked the frozen sadness that had locked Catherine's heart since the baby died. Now she would begin to heal.

Chapter 17

Rock Island Prison

Charlie shifted his weight from his aching leg. He stood alone in the damp, dreary Illinois weather, watching a group of prisoners. One prisoner seemed to be drawing a picture of another prisoner. Charlie looked closely at the artist, what was it about him that seemed so familiar. Suddenly, the man laughed and spoke to the person he was drawing. Charlie remembered Daniel's description of his friend from Louisiana. He had dark curly hair and an accent, and he could draw an amazing likeness of anyone. Charlie wondered if this man knew Daniel.

A guard entered the prison yard and called names for a work force. The name, Garth Beley, was called and Charlie observed the man was indeed Daniel's friend. As the prisoners prepared to leave the yard, Charlie fell into step with Garth.

"Hello, Garth. I'm Charlie Thornton, a friend of Daniel Woodall, and I believe you are also," Charlie said.

"You know Daniel. Is he here?" Garth asked.

"No, thank God. Daniel is not here," Charlie replied.

"Daniel was like a brother. We were separated during the Battle of Chickamauga and until now I didn't know if he survived that awful battle," Garth said.

Garth and Charlie worked on the railroad tracks all afternoon. When they parted, Garth slipped a large yellow apple into Charlie's coat pocket.

"Where did you ever get an apple in this place?" Charlie whispered.

"From a guard," Garth answered. "He brings me two food items every day. One day he brought his children to the fence and I drew their pictures. He has brought me food every day since. Eat the apple in the dark, people around here would kill you for an apple."

Charlie lay in the dark listening to the breathing of the other prisoners. When all were asleep, he bit into the fresh apple. "Oh, God, thank you for Garth and this apple," he prayed.

Three days passed before Charlie was in the yard with Garth. He saw him sitting alone on a bench and worked his way toward the bench and sank down beside Garth.

"Hi, Charlie, how are you?" he asked.

"I'm okay, just wanted to thank you," Charlie said.

"Hey, fellow, I'm glad to share with any friend of Daniel. I think he is the best man I ever met."

"I can sure agree with you on that," Charlie answered.

When Charlie's time was up in the yard, he stood up.

Garth whispered, "Move over in front of me."

As Charlie moved in front of Garth, he felt him drop something into his pocket. His mouth tingled as he remembered the tasty apple.

Charlie pulled the treasured food from his pocket and found that Garth had given him a large winter pear. When the other prisoners slept, he ate the pear. He fell asleep and dreamed of his Catherine; she was kneeling beside their bed praying for him. Then Garth appeared beside Catherine, smiling down on her. Had God sent Garth in answer to Catherine's prayers?

The next morning, Charlie remembered the dream and thought about it all day.

Charlie watched as two men carried the bodies of the men who had died in the night. They placed them side by side in a line. So many had died since the cold weather came. His heart seemed frozen as he looked at the horror of war. "Oh, God, let it end," he prayed. He wondered if one morning he, too, would be placed in the line and be buried here next to this awful prison, so far from his home.

Picking up his shovel, Charlie moved with the work gang to begin digging the graves that would receive the bodies of his fellow prisoners. His mind tried to perceive what it must be like for them now. Daniel had explained it to him so well. He said they would have spiritual bodies now, well and alive like Jesus in His resurrected body. Jesus had told his disciples, "I'm going to prepare a place for you." Charlie prayed all these men were now in heaven, where it would be warm and beautiful and they would not be hungry.

Charlie pulled his warm wool vest close around his body; he had loosened it while he dug. Thank God for the wool vest Catherine had knitted for him. He washed the grave dirt from his hands and entered the prison yard. Garth stood a few yards away watching him. He talked to other prisoners as he worked his way to Charlie.

"Bad day for you?" Garth asked.

"Yes, I guess we will all have a turn on that work gang," Charlie said.

"I've done it four times since I've been here," Garth replied.

As they talked, Charlie felt something drop into his pocket and then a second item dropped in. He thanked God for whatever it might be.

Late that night, Charlie drew from his pocket a boiled egg and a small crusty bread roll. Charlie remembered the boiled potato skins he had for his supper and thanked God for this very special food. He had been thankful for the potato peelings because there was nourishment for his body in potato peelings. His goal was to stay alive until this war was over so he could go home and tell Catherine and his boys about God. He wanted to tell them the way Daniel had told him. Before the war, he had never thought much about God. Now he knew God loved him very much. He would forever be indebted to Daniel for showing him his need of a savior.

The guard continued to bring Garth food and every time he saw Charlie he had something for him. One day, Charlie told him about his dream.

"Do you believe God has brought us to this place for a purpose?" Charlie asked.

"I never thought about God at all until I met Daniel. I always thought I could take care of myself, but Daniel simply lived and believed in God with all his heart. He never preached, he just believed God was working out good out of all these bad circumstances. Sometimes I have a hard time with that, but, yes, I believe we were meant to meet and God surely knows the reason why," Garth answered.

Charlie smiled and nodded his head. "Thanks, Garth," he said as he moved away. They actually spent very little time together. They never established set patterns or drew attention to themselves. They prayed for each other and worked together to survive.

The prisoners were gathered around two men fighting. One very young prisoner stood battered and bleeding against the wall. He clutched in one hand the dried end of a loaf of barley bread. Charlie edged closer to see the fighting men. One was the prison bully and the other was Garth. The bully was huge and expected everyone to give in to him. Garth was undoubtedly defending the bleeding youngster. He circled the bully and, giving a wild leap, he brought the bully crashing to the ground. In seconds, he wrapped his legs around him pinning him down. Then he wrapped his hands around the bully's throat and his eyes bulged from his head.

"Oh, God, don't let Garth kill the bully," Charlie prayed.

A prison guard appeared and the fight was over, both men were led away. The prisoners cheered for Garth as he left the yard, but Charlie knew he was in serious trouble for fighting. He also knew the bully would long remember the fight with the man who used to wrestle alligators.

Charlie prayed for Garth. He prayed the guard would still bring him food and that his time in the lock down cell would be short.

One week later, Garth and the bully were back in the prison yard.

There was no opportunity for Charlie to speak to Garth on his first day back, but on the second day he sat on the bench and hoped Garth would come.

"Hey, Charlie, I've missed you," Garth said. He smiled and sat down.

"I missed you, too, Garth and prayed much for you."

"I believe you did because fighting is usually a month lock up, but I think the prison commander knew that bully needed to be bullied a little bit himself."

"I thought you were going to kill him," Charlie said.

"I never intended to kill him, I just wanted him to know what it's like to be tortured, like he was torturing the young kid. Some people just have to learn the hard way," Garth said.

Charlie stood and passed in front of Garth. He felt two things drop into his pocket; indeed the guard was still on the job.

Christmas drew near and Charlie wished that he had something to give Garth. He pulled his wool vest close around his body as he shivered under his thin blanket at daybreak.

Many of the prisoners were sick. Small pox had spread thought the prison. Hundreds had died. Charlie now helped to dig trenches instead of individual graves. Burying the dead had become a full-time job.

Garth reached to pick up the shoulders of the next body, as he raised his head he looked into Charlie's eyes, a sad smile passed across his face.

"Hello, Charlie, I'm glad to see you don't have small pox."

"It's good to see you, Garth, I was worried about you."

"Sad news, my friend, the guard that provided the extra food has died of the small pox. His children are now infected, pray for the children. Another guard told me this morning. I saved this apple for you, it will be the last," Garth said, as he dropped a large red apple into Charlie's pocket.

Charlie and Garth buried fifty-three men in the trench that day. It was December 24, 1864. A light snow was falling as they bid each other good-bye.

Charlie washed in the cold wash barrel with a grimy bar of lye soap, which had been provided since the small pox came. He received his small portion of boiled dried beans and thanked God for them.

Using a sharp stick, Charlie cut his apple three ways to share with his cellmates, two men from South Carolina who had just arrived.

"Billy and Jim, I received an apple from outside the prison today and I want to share it with you for Christmas."

"An apple," Billy said.

"Yes, an apple God provided. It won't be much considering we all three will share it, but we will eat it slowly and thank God we have it."

"Thank you, Charlie, for sharing something so rare," Jim said.

"Oh, smell that wonderful smell, Christmas apples were always a special treat at our house, now it really does smell like Christmas," Billy said.

On a cold January morning, a buggy approached Rock Island Prison. A young woman drove the buggy. It was a rare sight to see a woman in this area. The woman stopped the buggy as a guard stood in the middle of the road.

"What brings you here, Ma'am?" the guard asked.

"I have come to see a prisoner," she said. "I would like to talk to a man named Garth Beley."

"That's impossible, Ma'am, you would never be allowed in the prison."

"Nothing is impossible, guard, take me to the man who is in charge of this prison," the woman said.

A guard came to Garth in the prison yard.

"You have a visitor," the guard said, "follow me."

Garth could not imagine a visitor in this awful place, but he followed the guard. He was led to a small, private room near the prison commander's office. A sad young woman sat waiting for him. She stood when Garth entered the room and extended her hand.

"I am Virginia Cole, wife of guard John Cole. You drew beautiful pictures of our children. I came to tell you that John and both the children have died of small pox. The pictures you drew of my children are all that I have now."

"I want you to know that guard, Matthew Dunn, will continue to bring you extra food. I have spoken to him, he was a close friend of John's and he will bring what extra food he can in his lunch each day. I will provide the food."

"Thank you so much for the pictures."

Garth stood with tears in his eyes and felt the awful pain of this young mother.

"I'm so glad I drew the pictures, Mrs. Cole, and I thank you for all the extra food that John brought and for whatever Matthew can bring, we have so little to eat."

The young woman left the room and a guard came and escorted Garth back to the prison yard.

Charlie sat on the bench and wondered where Garth was. Soon he saw Garth enter the yard and work himself through the prisoners.

"The children died, their mother came to tell me," Garth said.

"She also said she would continued to send us extra food by her husband's friend who is a guard."

"I'm so sorry the children died," Charlie said.

"I'm glad she has the pictures," Garth answered.

Chapter 18

Back to Atlanta

Daniel felt strange in his uniform; Marion had mended and pressed it and made it quite presentable. Nathaniel had provided him a coat to keep out the late January chill.

Daniel reached into his pocket, pulled out the map Nathaniel had made and studied it. He felt he could make it to Atlanta by the middle of February.

Daniel's heart was sad as he traveled across the farm lands and saw so much destruction. Many houses had been burned by the union army. People were kind to Daniel. He stopped and cut firewood or fixed fences in exchange for a hot meal and a little hay for Moses.

February 27, 1865, Daniel looked upon Atlanta and wept. The beautiful city lay in ruins. The thriving factories had been blown up by the confederate army to keep them from the union army. The railroad station was burned to the ground and the tracks ripped from the ground.

"Oh, God, have mercy on us all," Daniel prayed as he rode through the devastated city.

On the outskirts of town, some of the large old homes still stood. Daniel found a small unit of confederate soldiers. A sergeant seemed to be in charge of about twenty-five soldiers.

The sergeant came forward and said, "Welcome, I'm Howard Robinson."

Daniel shook the sergeant's hand and said, "I'm Daniel Woodall. I was fighting under General Hood and we were retreating. I was separated from my unit and left behind. A family found me near death and took me into their home."

"We are glad you have returned to Atlanta. The returning citizens have many needs and we have been able to help. A shortage of food is our greatest difficulty," the sergeant said.

"This house is our barrack, so far no civilian has returned to claim it. You will be on your own to find a space up the stairs and to the left. You may leave your belongings there. The kitchen is separate from the house, in the back. Supper will be served in an hour. You can put your mule in the corral across the road. Tomorrow, we will assign you to a work force; everyone has a turn on food detail," the sergeant continued.

As Daniel climbed the beautiful oak staircase, he thought about the family that had fled from this house. The door to the left led to a sunny room and he looked out on Peach Tree Street. The glass was still in the windows. All the windows on the first floor had been broken and were boarded up. Five makeshift beds and a few personal belongings were in the room.

An empty space against the back wall made a good spot for Daniel's feather quilt. He was so tired and longed to lie down and fall asleep. His hunger was greater than his tiredness and he knew if he slept he would get no supper. Taking his tin plate Marion had provided, he went in search of food.

Sergeant Robinson stood at the bottom of the stairs. "Come on, Daniel, let's see what the kitchen crew came up with today," he said.

Daniel followed the sergeant to the kitchen. In the middle of the kitchen stood two huge iron kettles built over a firebox and a large oven. Bubbling in the kettles was rabbit stew and from the oven the cook pulled pans of corn bread.

"Looks good to me," Daniel said. The soldiers lined up and supper was served.

After supper, the sergeant assigned work orders for the next day. Daniel was assigned to food detail.

He fell asleep that night with his belly full and his back warm, wrapped in the quilt.

Daylight streaked the eastern sky with a soft fusion of pink and gold. The blare of a bugle jarred Daniel from a sound sleep.

After a breakfast of corn bread crumbled in milk, Daniel met with four other soldiers on food detail. The cook was a chubby round-faced civilian. He had volunteered to cook for the soldiers if they would help the people. His name was Millard and he owned Millard's Restaurant in Atlanta, which burned down when the factories were destroyed. Millard hobbled on a clubfoot, therefore, he was never called to fight in the war.

Smiling broadly, Millard sat down at the table with the soldiers. The late February sun was warm on Daniel's back, as he listened to Millard's plan. "This is the right time of the year to go to the river fishing. The white perch come up from the deep water and they are really hungry. Take the food wagon and go fishing. I have prepared bait in this basket and the fishing poles are in the wagon."

Daniel sat on the wagon seat with Galen, the driver. He could hardly believe he was going fishing on this beautiful spring day. The mountain range in the distance glowed in the bright sunlight. The other soldiers sat on large tubs turned upside down.

"What happens tonight, Galen, if we don't catch any fish?" Daniel asked.

"Millard has lived in Atlanta all of his life, and he knows when things happen. I'll bet those fish will be biting," he said.

The Chattahoochee River lay still and peaceful as Daniel gazed upon it. Some civilians were already fishing. The soldiers watched as a shining perch split the water and landed on the riverbank.

The fishhooks were quickly baited and Daniel had never had so much fun fishing as he did that day. All of the tubs were filled by noon and off they hurried to get them cleaned for Millard.

Supper was a real celebration. Millard had jumped up and down when they returned, "I knew they would be biting," he cried.

Fresh fried perch and hush puppies were a rare treat. After the soldiers were fed, Millard served many civilians.

A lone horseman arrived in Atlanta on March 1st. He brought the news that in Washington on January 31, 1865, Congress voted 119 to 56 to pass the Thirteenth Amendment to abolish slavery. The amendment had been sent to the states for ratification. Daniel heard the news with great joy. He was glad that slavery would not be a part of America. The man also told them that on March 4th, Abraham Lincoln would be inaugurated for a second term. Daniel believed Lincoln to be a God-fearing, honest man and he hoped he could bring peace between the North and South.

Sweat poured down Daniel's face as he and Galen pulled a large beam into place on the house they were repairing. Sergeant Robinson shouted orders and led the work crew.

Tomorrow, they would start to rebuild Millard's Restaurant. Most of the structure had burned, but the soldiers had salvaged all the lumber they could from other buildings. After supper, Sergeant Robinson called for quiet and asked Millard to come from the kitchen. Millard arrived wondering why the sergeant wanted him outside.

"Millard, you have certainly done a great job cooking for us," the sergeant said.

A smile lit up Millard's face as the soldiers cheered.

"Now, we want you to know that we have been collecting material and tomorrow we are going to start rebuilding your restaurant," he continued.

Two large tears rolled down Millard's cheeks as the soldiers chanted," Tomorrow we build for Millard."

The azaleas bloomed early in April and the weather was beautiful. More people began to return to Atlanta.

Daniel stood on the top of Millard's Restaurant and watched as a group of horsemen rode fast into town.

"Confederate soldiers are coming," he cried.

All the soldiers waited as the rider approached.

One soldier yelled "The War Is Over! Lee has surrendered to Grant at Appomattox."

The soldiers burst into tears, fell to their knees and thanked God.

At supper, the story was told, General Lee, who had fought so long and valiantly for the confederacy, knew he was surrounded by union troops and he had no place to go. So, he had sent a note and a white towel into the union lines. One colonel proposed three cheers, but the union soldiers all broke down and cried, "Now we can go home."

Palm Sunday, April 19, 1865, General Lee arrived at the home of Wilmer McLean, the arranged meeting place. He was dressed in a crisp, gray uniform. He thought he would be Grant's prisoner and he wanted to look his best. Grant arrived in his mud-splattered uniform.

Colonel Eli Parker inscribed the articles of surrender for Lee and Grant to sign. The war was over; the confederate soldiers could keep their horses and guns and go home. Lee left the McLean home and mounted Traveler. His troops stood weeping when he returned.

"Boys," he said, "I have done the best I could for you. Go home now and if you make as good citizens as you have made soldiers, you will do well and I shall always be proud of you. Good-bye and God bless you all."

General Grant sent 25,000 rations of food to Lee's starving army that evening, a most generous, loving act of kindness.

The soldiers sat long around the supper table that night. They all agreed they would finish Millard's Restaurant and make plans to go home.

Daniel prayed as he lay upon his bed, "Thank you, God, the war is over. Soon I will go home to Catherine and we will raise up Joey in the United States of America, with no slavery."

Sergeant Robinson and Daniel pulled the long cross cut saw back and forth through the pine log, sweat covered their faces. The May sun was hot.

"Whoa, Daniel, you're wearing me out," Sergeant Robinson said.

While the sergeant and Daniel rested, the soldiers rolled another log into place and soon it was cut in half.

Another group of soldiers were busy chopping chairs from smaller logs. The cut boards would make tables.

Millard arrived with a cold bucket of water and a dipper. He handed Daniel the dipper and said, "I can't believe the restaurant is finished and you are making me tables and chairs."

The sergeant grinned and said, "Millard, you can't let your customers sit on the floor."

The last night the soldiers were together, supper was cooked and served in Millard's Restaurant. Catfish and collard greens were enjoyed by all.

Daniel patted Moses head and said, "Tomorrow, we start home." He was thankful he still had the little mule.

A loud commotion was going on in front of the barracks as Daniel came from the corral. A group of soldiers milled around the street on horses, six confederate officers and six union officers. Daniel stared in disbelief, they were traveling together. A confederate captain and a union captain swung from their horses and greeted Sergeant Robinson.

Daniel's heart skipped a beat as he thought, "Oh, my God, my God, it is Papa. He has survived the war."

Papa asked the sergeant where they might camp for the night.

"We are on a mission to Illinois to Rock Island Prison Camp to ensure that all Confederate prisoners are released," he said.

Captain Woodall had turned to mount his horse when he heard Daniel's cry, "Papa, Papa, I am here."

Racing toward each other, they embraced as all the soldiers cheered. Everyone rejoiced that father and son had been reunited.

"Papa, I'm so glad you are here," Daniel said, "We almost missed each other. I was leaving for home in the morning. I have a mule in the corral that was a gift from another soldier and I was leaving at daybreak."

"It would be dangerous traveling alone, son. There is still killing and looting in many places. Come with me to Rock Island Prison, then we will go home together."

Moses and Daniel's gun were traded for Sergeant Robinson's horse.

"Captain Lance, my son Daniel will be coming with us," Papa said.

"Welcome, Daniel, I see you have a fine horse," the captain replied.

Chapter 19

Daniel Comes to Rock Island Prison

The sun rose large and red like a giant balloon on that morning in late May. The soldiers were mounted and Captain Lance gave the command to move out.

Daniel thought of all the times he had left Atlanta. He did not look forward to going to Rock Island Prison, he had heard the horror stories of how many prisoners had starved and died in the prisons both in the north and in the south. Papa rode beside him, determined to carry out the last orders he had been given by the confederate army.

The soldiers rode hard, each man anxious to complete his military service and go home. They covered 25 to 30 miles a day. Sometimes, they stayed in small towns; other times they camped along the way.

Just outside Chattanooga, Daniel sat on his horse looking down into a sea of black faces. He felt great compassion, they were like children surging around the union soldiers, singing "Freedom, freedom, thank God for freedom."

Captain Lance asked, "Who is in charge here?"

A large black man walked through the crowd; he stood head and shoulder over most of the other people.

"Hello, sir, my name is Seth, this is my home. I own ten acres of land. I have been free for 12 years. My master freed me when I saved his young son from drowning and gave me this land. Most of these people have just been freed, they came from the south and don't know what to do. I am trying to help them. Right now, our biggest problems are food and sanitation. The group next to the woods is building outhouses. The ones behind the house are building brush arbors to sleep under."

"Well, Seth, you sure have your work cut out for all of you. We wish you well in your endeavors," Captain Lance said.

Papa said, "The freed black slaves are a lot like the Hebrew slaves that were freed from slavery in Egypt. I pray President Lincoln has a plan because the black people will have a great struggle before they are really free."

The days passed and most of the time the weather was warm and pleasant. When the soldiers reached Illinois, they were happy. Tomorrow they would reach Rock Island Prison.

Captains Lance and Woodall led the soldiers to the prison gate.

Daniel looked upon the prison with a deep sadness as he saw the wretchedness of this place. He wondered how many confederate soldiers had died and if he would know any of the prisoners.

The prison gate swung open and the soldiers were escorted to the prison commandant's office.

Captain Lance spoke first, "We have come to inform you that the War Between the States is over. Captain Woodall and I have been commissioned by General Grant to inform you that all the prisoners in this place are to be released to go home."

Pulling an official letter from his uniform, he waited for the commandant to read the order.

"Now, pass the order through the prison, Captain Woodall and I will do an inspection. We will need all your records of the dead. The food you have will be divided up among the prisoners for their journey home. The sick men will be cared for in town until they are able to travel."

The fat little commandant climbed the prison tower and called for attention. He announced to the prisoners, "The war is over, you are all free." A great cry rose up from the prisoners. Many fell to their knees, thanking God and weeping.

Charlie and Garth buried the last soldier. Only two had died last night. Slowly they followed the guards back to the prison. As they neared the prison, they heard a loud cry.

"It must be a rebellion," the guard cried. "Come on, run."

Reaching the prison gate, they all stopped in amazement. The prison gate stood open and prisoners streamed through the gate crying, "The war is over and we are free."

"The war is over," Charlie whispered to Garth, "Can you believe the war is really over? I can go home to Catherine and the boys." With tears streaming down his cheeks, Charlie walked through the open gate into the prison and Garth followed.

Daniel sat on his horse with the other soldiers waiting for the captains to return from the commandant's office. Today was June 20, 1865, he would long remember this day. His eyes traveled over the men, dirty, ragged and starved almost to skin and bone. Slowly, his eyes focused on two men walking into the prison.

Leaping from his horse, Daniel raced through the prisoners flinging himself into the arms of Charlie and Garth.

"Daniel," they cried, "Oh, God, was it you, Daniel, who brought the news that the war is over?"

"It was Papa and a union captain who were given the order to come here and make sure all confederate prisoners are released. I am traveling with them. Papa found me in Atlanta," Daniel answered.

"You were still in Atlanta?" Charlie asked.

"No, Charlie, I had returned to Atlanta. I will tell you the whole story later," Daniel replied.

That night, a pot of dried beans and salt pork was cooked over a campfire. Charlie and Garth slept full and warm on Daniel's feather quilt.

The sun was hot and a few fluffy clouds floated across the blue sky the day Papa, Daniel, Charlie and Garth left Rock Island, Illinois going home. They traveled at a slow pace, since the horses carried a double load.

Daniel was surprised at how much rebuilding had been accomplished in Atlanta.

"Sergeant Robinson, how are you?" Daniel called to his friend.

"I'm good, my friend, I see you and your Papa have had a good trip," he said.

"I thought you would have gone home by now."

"No, I've decided to stay on here and help these folks rebuild Atlanta. Millard has given me a room in the restaurant and we are faring well," the sergeant said.

When the sergeant found out that Garth didn't have a wife and children, he persuaded him to stay and help rebuild Atlanta. An instant friendship had sprung up between them.

Laughing, Sergeant Robinson said to Daniel, "Some day, we will be famous in this town. I'm going to get my self elected sheriff and Garth will paint pictures of wealthy Atlanta families."

Charlie met some Alabama soldiers on their way home. They had a wagon pulled by two mules and they invited Charlie to come with them.

"Some day when there are railroads and trains again, I will bring my Catherine to meet your Catherine," Charlie said as he hugged Daniel and Papa good-bye.

The last night in Atlanta was celebrated in Millard's Restaurant. They had a fine dinner of fried fish and fresh new potatoes cooked with green peas in a white sauce.

"Millard, you have outdone yourself," Daniel said, smiling at the little man as he bustled around the restaurant serving his customers.

Chapter 20

How Long, Oh Lord, How Long?

Joey lay on his stomach playing with his farm. A cold rain fell outside as Catherine hung their clothes around the stove to dry. She disliked hanging wash in the house, but it had rained for days and she had no choice.

Shaking the water from his coat, James called, "Is supper just about ready?"

"Yes," Catherine answered.

Catherine dished up the chicken and dumplings. They had started eating the laying hens because meat was so scarce. She had cured pork yet, but she knew it must be stretched for months. Sweet potatoes, winter squash, cabbage and carrots made up the majority of their foods. Thank God they had a good harvest in the fall and James had stored the vegetable in a straw-lined underground hole.

No news about the war had been heard for a long time. Where Papa and Daniel were was unknown. Catherine prayed they were alive.

The February rains gave way to spring. The dandelion greens and watercress were in abundance. Joey and Catherine gathered them daily. There was something about the bitter greens that brought color back to their cheeks.

James came from the barn and washed up for supper. Catherine served fresh greens seasoned with pork and sweet potatoes.

"We have to think about getting cotton seed," Catherine said.

"I know, tomorrow I will go to the gin and talk to Mr. Lelland. Perhaps he will give me seed charged against the cotton he is still holding."

"Sometimes I wonder if we should even try to grow cotton this year," James said.

"Yes, I thought about that also, but perhaps the war will be over soon and the north will need our cotton again. If we don't plant cotton, the fields will be overgrown with weeds and that wouldn't be good," Catherine answered.

"You're right, we must continue to work the farm as best we can," James agreed.

"Good morning, Mr. Lelland," James called as he pushed open the office door. "Do you have any cotton seed to sell? I don't have any money. I thought maybe you could let me have some seed against the bales of cotton you are holding," James continued.

Shaking his head, the owner of the gin said, "Sorry, James, I have no cotton seeds. I only had a few hundred pounds and they went early in February. The only seed I have is rye; if it grows well, you could harvest it and grind it into rye flour for bread next winter."

James accepted the bags of rye seed and Mr. Lelland marked the cost in his books.

"Just plow up the ground and sow the seed, James. Lots easier than growing cotton. You can't eat cotton," he said.

By mid-April, James and Mama's rye fields were emerald green. The slender stiff stalks waved in the gentle breeze. James hoped it would produce many bushels of grain.

Mama and Charlie arrived early one morning, they were going to Warm Springs so Mama could purchase a block of brown sugar.

"What can I bring you, Catherine?" Mama asked.

"Oh, Mama, I have no money and I can't expect you to buy for us," Catherine cried.

"Listen, Catherine, you are my family. What we have belongs to all of us. Now, make you list and I will buy what I can with the money I have," Mama said.

Charlie stayed to play with Joey and James drove the buggy to town.

A large group of people was gathered in front of Mr. Blagg's General Store everyone seemed to be talking at once.

"I wonder what is going on," James said.

Mr. Blagg saw them coming and ran to meet them.

"Elizabeth, James, wonderful news, the war is over," he called.

Mama had started to step from the buggy, she sank back to the seat and burst into tears.

"Oh, thank you, God, now Billie and Daniel can come home," she cried.

While Mama selected the things she and Catherine needed, James listened to the man from Oglethorpe who had brought the news that the war was over. General Lee had surrendered to General Grant. The Confederate States of America were no more.

Catherine sat on the porch steps in the warm May sun. Joey and Charlie chased the twine ball around the flowerbed. Several red roses bloomed on the rose bush. She thought of Daniel's love in building the flowerbed and planting the rose bush.

The buggy rolled into view. Catherine thought, "James is driving so much faster than usual." She hoped nothing was wrong.

Mama jumped from the buggy and ran to Catherine, "The war is over, Lee has surrendered to Grant," she cried.

Tears of joy streamed down their faces as they held each other and thought of the homecoming.

Mama and Charlie stayed for supper and they talked long.

"All the slaves have been freed, where do you suppose they will go? They have no food, money or homes," James said.

"It will be a long time before all the problems of this war are solved," Mama answered.

The next morning, James opened the kitchen door. One look at his white face told Catherine something was wrong.

"What, James?" she cried out.

"A black woman and two little children are sleeping in the hay mound. I went to get hay and there they were, sound asleep," James said.

"Oh, they must be freed slaves," Catherine said. "They will be so hungry." Hurrying to Joey's door, she checked to make sure he was still sleeping. "I will come with you, we don't want to frighten them."

Catherine opened the barn door, a bright shaft of sunlight lit up the hay mound. The young woman jumped to her feet, trying to hide her children and their belongings, wrapped in a quilt. The little boy hid his head behind his mother; the little girl stuck her head covered with tiny pigtails out to look at Catherine.

"It's okay," Catherine said, "We will help you." Smiling she moved toward the woman, "Are you traveling alone with the children?"

"Yes, ma'am, I'm trying to get to Oglethorpe. Could you give us something to eat? We are very hungry," the woman said.

"Come to the house and we will make breakfast," Catherine said.

The woman took the children to the outhouse and Catherine hurried to the kitchen.

James went to the well and brought the cold milk. He poured glasses of milk and passed them to the family. Catherine added corn meal to the boiling water on the stove and soon had steaming bowls of mush on the table.

Joey ran into the kitchen and stopped in startled amazement when he saw the little black twins. He hid behind Catherine and peered out.

"Who are they?" he asked. He had never seen a black person.

The mother said, "Hello, little one, I'm Jenna and these are my children, Harriet and Henry."

Catherine lifted Joey into his chair.

"This is Joey," she said, laughing at his observation of the twins. "He will be four years old this month."

"My children will be four in July," Jenna said.

"After breakfast, you may go outside and play with the twins. Won't that be fun?" Catherine asked.

"Tell us about you and the children, Jenna, where have you come from?" Catherine asked.

Jenna's curly black hair lay in ringlets and her smoky black eyes were sad in her pretty face as she looked at Catherine.

"I'm from a plantation in South Georgia, ma'am. We rode on a wagon with other people who were trying to get to the north, but they were going in a different direction so I had to leave them. I have to go to Oglethorpe. I was a cook for Mrs. Presley on Presley Ridge Plantation. My husband, Isaac, was the butler, but times got very hard and Mrs. Presley sold my husband to a Mr. Davon who owns a hotel in Oglethorpe. I pray I can find him," Jenna said.

Tears smarted in Catherine's eyes as she felt the pain Jenna had suffered.

James had listened while Jenna talked. Jumping up in excitement, he exclaimed, "Catherine, I remember Daniel told us about Isaac who worked in the hotel. Papa and Daniel stayed in the Davon Hotel and there was a black man name Isaac. That was over a year ago, but perhaps he is still there."

"Oh, thank you, God. I pray he is still there," Jenna said.

"I'll do the dishes, ma'am," Jenna said. "Thank you so much for sharing your food with us."

"You're welcome, Jenna, thank you for doing the dishes. I'll dress Joey so the children can go play," Catherine said.

Joey wiggled in excitement as Catherine dressed him. He so seldom had children to play with.

"Come on," Joey called to the twins who still sat in their chairs at the table.

Looking at their mother for approval, they jumped from their seats. Laughing and jostling each other, they ran outside.

"You had better go along to supervise, James," Catherine said.

"Thank you, Miss Catherine, for being so good to us," Jenna said, "we must leave early in morning."

Catherine and Jenna were rolling out the sweet potato dough they were making biscuits from, for Jenna's trip.

"Jenna, we will miss you and the twins. James will take you in the wagon to our friend who lives on the other side of Warm Springs. You can stay with her overnight and leave early the next morning. You will have only ten miles to reach Oglethorpe. I hope you can get another ride," Catherine said.

"God will watch over us," Jenna answered.

Catherine packed all the sweet potato biscuits in a clean flour sack. They would feed Jenna and the twins for several days.

"'Bye, Miss Catherine," Harriet and Henry called.

They tumbled about on the quilt Catherine had spread on the bottom of the wagon. Joey stood to kiss his mama good-bye since he had been allowed to go with James.

"Thank you, again, for your kindness," Jenna said, as she hugged Catherine good-bye and climbed up on the wagon seat with James.

Catherine sat on the front steps in the quiet morning and thought of Daniel. The war was over, the slaves were free. Soon, Daniel would come home. The rye stalks swayed in the breeze and she thought how pretty the fields were. Daniel would be pleased that she and James had planted a crop.

The sun was dropping in the late afternoon sky when James and Joey returned.

James pulled the wagon near the porch and called to Catherine, "Miss Jenny sends her love and said to tell you she will take good care of Jenna and the twins. Tomorrow, they will go on to Oglethorpe. Joey is sound asleep. I'll bring him inside. He is so tired from playing so hard with the twins."

Joey rolled over to his side and smiled when James laid him in bed.

A flash of lightening and a loud crash of thunder awakened Catherine from a sound sleep. She sat up in bed, listening to the rain lashing against the house. The summer rain would be good for the crops and cool down the hot July weather.

As the storm rage outside, Catherine thought of Daniel. Why didn't he come home? The war had been over for three months and each day she had thought he would come. Nagging thoughts plagued her. He's dead, he's not coming back. She pushed the terrible thoughts from her mind, praying the prayer she had prayed the day he left her, "Please, God, hold me up and bring him back to me."

Catherine laid her head upon her pillow and dreamed while she slept. A grave stood open and ready to receive the body of her loved one and she cried in her dream "No, No" and rushed forward with a quilt to cover the open grave. When she opened her eyes from the dream, she clutched the quilt to her heart and cried.

July 27, 1865 dawned bright and beautiful. Catherine bent low to cut the okra into her basket and pick the fat green butter beans. Joey played under the maple tree, swinging on the swing James had made.

James watched Catherine, she cleaned, cooked and cared for Joey and he knew her thoughts were "Would Daniel ever return?" It was the same with Mama waiting for Papa.

Catherine called, "Come on in the house, boys, supper is ready."

Heads bowed and hands joined, they were thanking God for their food when the sound of horses coming stopped their prayer. Jumping from their chairs, they raced to the porch. Two riders rode into the yard.

Daniel and Papa jumped from their horses, embracing them all.

Catherine thought her heart would burst with happiness as Daniel swept her into his arms crying, "My Beloved, I am home at last."

The End